FRANK J. DERFLER, JR., a communications manager with the United States Department of Defense, has published several articles in magazines and journals related to technology and computer systems. He currently writes a monthly column about microcomputer-based data systems for Kilobaud Microcomputing magazine.

Microcomputer Data Communication Systems

Frank J. Derfler, Jr.

A SPECTRUM BOOK
PRENTICE-HALL, INC., Englewood Cliffs, New Jersey 07632

Library of Congress Cataloging in Publication Data

Derfler, Frank J.
  Microcomputer data communication systems.

  "A Spectrum Book."
  Includes index.
  1. Data transmission systems. 2. Microcomputers.
I. Title.
TK5105. D48   001.64'404   81-17725
                             AACR2

ISBN 0-13-580720-4

ISBN 0-13-580712-3 {PBK.}

Editorial/production supervision by Louise M. Marcewicz
Cover design by Jeannette Jacobs
Manufacturing buyer: Cathie Lenard

10 9 8 7 6 5 4 3 2 1

Prentice-Hall International, Inc., London
Prentice-Hall of Australia Pty. Limited, Sydney
Prentice-Hall of Canada, Ltd., Toronto
Prentice-Hall of India Private Limited, New Delhi
Prentice-Hall of Japan, Inc., Tokyo
Prentice-Hall of Southeast Asia Pte. Ltd., Singapore
Whitehall Books Limited, Wellington, New Zealand

For Marlene and Shandra: Thank you for the time.

Contents

Acknowledgments

Many terms used in this book are the registered trademarks of various corporations or individuals. Here are the most common terms used:

APPLE II: Apple Computer, Inc.
ASCII Express: Bill Blue and Southwestern Data Systems
CAT: Novation, Inc.
CP/M: Digital Research, Inc.
Crosstalk: Microstuf, Inc.
Dumb Terminal: Lear Siegler, Inc.
Horizon: North Star Computers, Inc.
H-89: Heath Company
LYNX: Emtrol Systems, Inc.
Microconnection: Microperipheral Corporation
MICROMODEM II: Hayes Microcomputer Products
MNET: CompuServe
North Star: North Star Computers, Inc.
OMNITERM: Lindbergh Systems
PET: Commodore Business Machines, Inc.
REACH: The Software Toolworks
Smartmodem: Hayes Microcomputer Products
Source: Source Telecomputing Corp.
ST80, ST80-CC, ST80-PBB, ST80-X10: Lance Micklus, Inc.
TRS-80: Tandy Corporation
Z-TERM: Bill Blue and Southwestern Data Systems
Z80: Zilog, Inc.

chapter one

Introduction

We are in the middle of humanity's second great information explosion. The first great explosion came with the invention of movable metal type. The second great explosion is being fueled by the marriage of computers and communications. Many experts believe the availability of inexpensive data communication systems will make as large an impact on our culture as did the development of the printing press in the fifteenth century. More things have been invented since World War II than during the total prior history of mankind. Information pours out of newspapers, books, and electronic media, but the individual often finds that this information must be arranged in a usable form and transmitted in a timely manner if it is to be useful. Sorting, arranging, and transmitting information are the strong features of data communication systems.

Figure 1-1. Development of data communication through the ages.

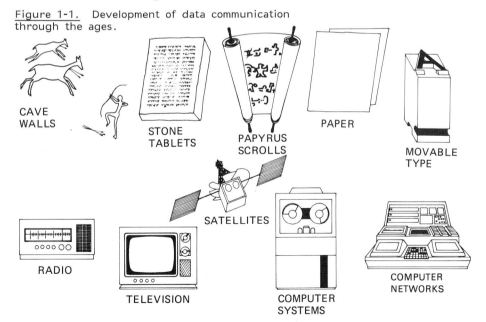

CAVE WALLS

STONE TABLETS

PAPYRUS SCROLLS

PAPER

MOVABLE TYPE

RADIO

TELEVISION

SATELLITES

COMPUTER SYSTEMS

COMPUTER NETWORKS

THE MICROCOMPUTER: A COMMUNICATIONS DOORWAY

If you own a microcomputer, you have the prime element in a data communications terminal. It can allow you access to the world's information when and how you want it. On a practical level, giving your microcomputer a communications capability can make it easy to transfer programs from one system to another--even if the systems have different disk or cassette storage devices. On a broader scope, a microcomputer acting as a terminal can bring in current news, transportation schedules, shopping and stocks information, and mail--at the speed of light.

The information network we used until the early 1980s had not changed much since the 1930s. It was based on the newspaper and supplemented by magazines, telephones, radio, and, later, television. This sort of network ties its users into certain conditions. The major condition or prerequisite for receiving information from the network is this: You must be connected to the network at the specific time the information is being sent. You must get the right issue of the newspaper to read the story you want. You must be ready to listen to or watch the evening news at the time it is being transmitted or you will miss the item you want to see. You must be ready to answer the telephone within the 30-second period of the typical seven-ring attempted call or you will not be connected. Studies show that the number of successfully completed telephone calls in the business world is regularly as low as a miserable 15%. The demand that you be plugged into the system at the right time to receive a transmitted message is a kind of tyranny. I refer to it as the "Time Tyranny of Telecommunications."

Figure 1-2.   The Time Tyranny of Telecommunications.

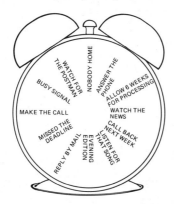

THE TYRANNY OF TIME

A great deal of research and money has been spent on products to break the Time Tyranny of Telecommunications. Telephone answering machines and video tape recorders are devices that automatically

connect into the network at the right time and save the transmitted messages until you are ready to play them back. They act
as a kind of storage buffer between you and the distribution
network. They buffer, or hold, the information until you are
ready to receive it, but the network still transmits or broadcasts
the information only when it is convenient or expedient for the
individuals who provide the information. The network does not
know or care if the user is ready to listen.

A more modern approach is through modification of the network
itself. The information network can be changed so that it becomes
an interactive system instead of just a broadcast into the blind.
Information (messages, orders, news, sports, and so on) is loaded
into an interactive system at the convenience of the information
provider. The system delivers that information at the convenience
of the information receiver and in the order and format suiting
his needs.

These modern networks take many forms. Several telephone
companies now provide centralized storage of voice messages.
Voice messages are digitally recorded and played back when the
person to whom they are addressed checks into his central mailbox
Voice message storage systems do not require any specialized
equipment to send and receive, but the messages cannot be sorted,
filed, or stored by the receiver in any easy way. The most
effective modern information networks or systems can do all these
things and more.

Three general kinds of systems are becoming popular: electronic message systems, information utilities, and teletext
systems.

ELECTRONIC MESSAGE SYSTEMS

There are many kinds of electronic message systems. Among them
are Computer Bulletin Board Systems (CBBS), Apple Bulletin Board
Systems (ABBS), Forum 80 systems, PET Message Systems, and others.
All these systems operate in a similar manner, but they differ in
the hardware and software used by the central computer and in the
specific features they may provide.

Physically, an electronic message system is usually a standard microcomputer from one of the popular manufacturers. The
computer probably has 48K (kilobytes) or more of random access
memory and several disk drives. Most importantly, it has a device called an auto-answer modem. A modem (which will be
described more thoroughly in Chapter 3) is a device that converts
the electrical output of a computer or terminal into audio tones
which can be transmitted and received over standard telephone
lines. This modem picks up or "answers" the telephone line when
it rings. The caller on the distant end is automatically
connected to the computer that is running the message system
program.

Message system programs differ in detail, but they usually
perform several standard functions. They normally ask the caller
first to complete a sign-on routine for purposes of identifica-
tion. The sign-on routine may include many details such as name,

location, and telephone number of the caller, or it may be as
simple as a coded serial number transmitted automatically by the
caller's microcomputer terminal.

After the sign-on, the message program gives the user several
options. The first microcomputer-based message systems were
little more than places where users could "pin up" notes to their
friends. The most advanced systems now allow their users to run
programs, play games, use higher order programming languages
(such as Pascal), keep private "mailboxes," read interesting articles or editorials, order products from other users, and exchange programs with the host system. These services are usually
provided free of charge. Often they are operated by private
individuals, but many businesses selling computer products have
found that a message system is a valuable link to their customers.

INFORMATION UTILITIES

Would you like to have the complete reports of a national news
wire service in your home? Would you like to have stock market
reports, business analyses, government publications, home and
garden articles, shopping tips, merchandise ordering, train and
airline schedules, and mail service at your fingertips? Would
you also like to have the option of using programs requiring
large memories and programming languages not normally available
on a microcomputer? Information utilities can provide you with
all these capabilities and more.

Information utilities are a specialized form of what has been
known for years as time sharing services. In a time sharing
service, a large central computer--or often a cluster of medium-
sized computers--serves customers in remote locations over telephone lines. The service allows each customer to feel as if the
computer is dedicated to him alone. The time sharing services
entering the information utility market have provided some very
unique programs for their customers to run. These programs
provide the kinds of "electronic Sunday newspaper" and reference
library services described above.

Your microcomputer can be used as an access device to these
information utilities. A communicating microcomputer can enhance
the operation of these subscription services by saving information
and files locally, preparing messages and files for transmission to
the bigger system, and speaking to the bigger system in quick
shorthand codes.

Two major information utilities are marketing their services
especially for microcomputer users. The Source is the name of one
service provided by Source Telecomputing Corporation in
McLean, Virginia. A competing service is marketed by CompuServe
of Columbus, Ohio. Both of these services are described in detail
in Chapter 11. While the Source and CompuServe compete with each
other, they both face growing competition from another form of
information utility: teletext and videotext services.

TELETEXT AND VIDEOTEXT

Teletext and videotext systems also provide interactive delivery of information into the homes and offices of their subscribers. Since their services are not designed especially for microcomputer users, I will not spend much time describing them. However, anyone interested in data communications should understand basically how these systems work and what their impact might be.

Teletext and videotext are both centered on the same kind of centralized information-loaded computer used by the information utilities. These systems rely on terminal devices that are more common in the home than are microcomputers.

Teletext uses the home telephone line and a specially modified television set to link the subscriber to the central computer. The typical user has a small keypad which allows selections from displayed menus. The central computer is informed of the selection by a short message transmitted over the telephone line from the television terminal. The selected page of information is sent from the central computer to the home user over the telephone line at a high rate of speed.

Videotext also uses a modified television set, but not the telephone line. The pages of information are transmitted by a local television station during idle milliseconds in the regular transmission signal. The information is sent in short high-speed bursts repeated in a regular pattern. Videotext is not truly an interactive system. There are no transmissions from the television terminal to the central computer. Instead, the user's television set waits for the desired page of information to be transmitted; then it captures and displays it. This wait is usually less than a minute.

Videotext and teletext systems are similar to information utilities, but they aim at slightly different markets. Videotext and teletext want to serve the average American family at home. Information utilities are probably aimed at more sophisticated users at home and in business. Both videotext and teletext systems make use of graphic color displays. They provide information quickly and in standard formats. They are simple to use, but they lack the flexibility and power gained from teaming centralized information utilities with remote microcomputer terminals.

TRANSMISSION SYSTEMS

The new modern interactive information networks are possible only because of the availability of modern transmission systems. Transmission systems carry the electronic messages between the communicating microcomputers and the terminals or computers to whom they are talking. The only pieces of the transmission systems we normally think of or see are the home telephone instruments and the wires going from pole to pole. These instruments and local wires are common to all the systems we use, but after our voice or the computer modem tone leaves the local telephone office, it may go by many routes.

Frequently, users of electronic message systems find they make many long distance telephone calls to get on the systems interesting to them. The cost of these calls can mount quickly. The most common long distance routes are those provided by American Telephone and Telegraph. Over the past few years, however, some competition has developed due to the deregulation of the telecommunications industry in the United States. This means you may be able to call long distance more cheaply by using an alternative to the traditional telephone service. Two such companies are competing strongly in providing this service.

Southern Pacific Communications offers a service called "Sprint" to private customers. MCI Communications Corporation was the first company to challenge the American Telephone and Telegraph monopoly in long distance communications: their service is known as Execunet. In Chapter 11, the geographic areas served by these carriers--and the rate structures--will be described. This is important information for the microcomputer communicator who wants to use electronic message systems around the country.

The information utilities also make use of special communications carriers to route the great volume of data they transmit and receive. Tymnet and Telenet are two telecommunications networks especially dedicated to computer communications. Carriers dedicated to a special purpose such as data communications are called value-added carriers because of the message processing, error detection and correction, and other specialized services they provide. These networks are not normally noticed by information utility users, but they function in very special ways to connect digital communications systems.

Finally, the spread of cable television services and the possibility of direct satellite transmissions are creating new opportunities for videotext and modified teletext services. Several two-way cable television systems are operating around the country with exciting results. Presidential candidates, local elected officials, and professional athletic coaches have all experienced the instant feedback of two-way cable.

THE DIGITAL DATA FUTURE

Data communications networks are rapidly changing the way we conduct our lives. These networks have made a tremendous impact on banking, publishing, travel, and government services. The microcomputer in your home or office can be an important part of one or several data networks. Opening the door to the information explosion is an easy and pleasant thing to do. The following chapters will give you the technical and practical keys to microcomputer communications.

chapter two

The Fundamentals

It is not necessary to understand the internal combustion engine in order to drive a car; similarly it is not necessary to understand anything technical about data communications to use an electronic message system or information utility. Knowing what is going on "under the hood," however, can greatly increase your enjoyment and possibly reduce maintenance and repair bills. Some technical understanding is also needed when you are trying to customize your own machine.

SERIAL DATA

The data transmission systems used by microcomputers are referred to as serial systems. This means that data comes out bit by bit in a serial stream, rather than--the way some printers and other devices are fed--by the parallel transmission of eight bits of data simultaneously. The telephone line is not a big enough creek bed to hold the wide wash of parallel transmission, so we will concentrate on the serial stream. Let's start at the headwaters of all data and float on down.

Every microcomputer has some input and output ports. The keyboard feeds an input port and the video monitor or RF modulator receives signals from an output port. The cassette or disk controller moves data both in and out and is therefore called an I/O port. It is possible to use the cassette port of most microcomputers to communicate over limited distances by connecting the audio signals to the telephone lines. This can only be done with two identical model computers, however, because cassette systems are not standard. But even when identical computers are used, the cassette coding system is very sensitive to the changes imposed on the signal by the telephone circuit. Many computer users experience problems trying to load programs from a local recorder. Minor changes in audio level or the phase of the signal can make loading difficult. These problems are compounded when telephone lines are used. Use of the cassette port as a communications port can be a very limited and frustrating way to try and communicate.

RS-232-C

A standard and practical I/O coding scheme is needed for long distance data communications. Computers communicate internally and
externally in digital signals. Inside every system, direct
current voltages are being switched from high to low voltage many
times a second. These changes in voltage represent digital bits
of information. However, the voltages used differ between the
systems. Even in the microcomputer family, different microprocessors are different voltage levels. If all systems are to
communicate on a common network, some standard for external voltage levels must be set. We need a solid definition of the electrical standards to be used. This has been supplied by the Electronic Industries Association (EIA): standard code RS-232-C.
Outside the United States this code is known as the Consultive
Committee International Telephone and Telegraph (CCITT) code V.24.
This code provides a common description of what the signal coming
out of and going into the serial port will look like electrically.
Specifically, RS-232-C provides for a signal swinging from a
nominal +12 to a nominal -12 volts at certain specified current
levels and resistive loads.

Table 2-1. RS-232-C Electrical Standards

Signal Name	Logic	Control State	Electrical Parameter
MARK	ONE	OFF	-24 TO + 3 VOLTS
SPACE	ZERO	ON	+3 TO + 24 VOLTS

    The RS-232-C electrical standard limits the length of the
connecting cable to fifty feet. In practice, cables many times
that length can be used if they are routed away from appliances
and other sources of electrical interference. The timing signals
used in synchronous transmission are particularly susceptible to
noise.
    The voltage area between +3 and -3 volts is a transition
area, and signals should not rest in this zone or they will cause
erratic operation of the logic circuits. The positive and
negative signals do not have to be of the same amplitude. Positive voltages of 12 volts and negative voltages of -5 or -18
volts are commonly found working together. The change in voltage
state is the actual signaling function. The standard also defines
the cables and connectors used to connect data communications
devices together. This will become quite important when we discuss the hook-up of actual hardware. Using this standard code
simplifies the job of getting information in and out of a
computer, terminal, or peripheral device. A new standard, called
RS-449, has been adopted which will eventually be a replacement
or an alternative to RS-232-C, but compatibility with RS-232-C is
specified in RS-449. RS-232-C will continue to be a useful
signaling standard for many years to come.

The terms commonly used with electrical coding standards may be confusing. They are often carried over from other systems, but once you get them straight, they are easy to understand. Because of the peculiarities of solid state logic devices, a logic state called "0" may not indicate zero volts. Indeed, just the opposite is true. A logic state of 0 is defined as the positive voltage (+3 to +25 volts) signal in RS-232-C. This is also known as a space signal. "Space" and "mark" are two designations held over from the days of mechanical printers, which are operated by electromagnets and driven by direct current circuits. If you read any literature stating that a space should be transmitted, you know you are looking for a positive voltage or a 0 logic state.

The logic state of "1" is just the opposite. A logical 1 is a negative direct current voltage; it is also known as a mark. You may wish to remember the phrase, "The teacher gave the student a low mark, but a logical one."

The change in the direct current voltage level serves as the signal or bit of information in the RS-232-C system. These bits are sensed, counted, and stored by data communications devices. The direct current voltages used in this interconnection system can travel about fifty feet before they lose their important electrical characteristics. RS-232-C signaling is not used directly for long distance communications, but it is used to connect microcomputers with modems. RS-232-C is the most commonly used standard for local connection of microcomputers, terminals, and modems.

RS-232-C is, however, just an electrical standard. It defines the voltage swings and other electrical parameters. It does not define what the voltage swings mean in terms of intelligent information. It is as if we said we will all use red and blue flags for signaling, but we did not define what the position of the flags will mean. Another standard--a coding standard--is needed.

ASCII

The most commonly used coding standard is the American Standard Code for Information Exchange, or ASCII. ASCII is actually a data alphabet. Internationally, it is known as CCITT Alphabet Number 5. This alphabet not only tells us the coding of the electrical signals that make up the characters in ASCII, but it provides useful numeric values for the characters, and special standards for recording information on punch cards and magnetic media such as tape. ASCII defines the standard keyboard and provides codes for the smooth processing of information over data transmission systems.

ASCII defines certain coded signals as control codes. These are codes that usually mean something special to a machine. Control codes may tell electronic printers to tab, ring a bell, or begin a new page. They may stop the running of a computer program or turn on a tape drive. Control codes are valuable in data communication systems because of the flexibility they provide. The availability of control codes is of particular interest to microcomputer users because some microcomputer hardware and software combinations do not have the ability to transmit control codes when operating as terminals. Such systems would be severely limited when operating with certain message systems or running programs on computer time sharing services.

The coding of an ASCII character is easy to understand. The code essentially signifies how many times and when a voltage or tone goes high or low in a seven-bit sequence. The capital letter A, for instance, has a coding of 1000001. This would be coded over a piece of wire by sending one negative voltage (remember, a logic state of 1 is a negative voltage in RS-232-C signaling), five positive voltage pulses, and a final negative voltage pulse within certain time slots set by internal clocks in the equipment. Over a telephone line, the direct current voltages would be converted to audio tones by a modem. The coding of the audio tones for the letter A would be one low tone, five high tones, and one low tone. This coding is also a number in the binary (base 2) number system. If the binary value is converted to the decimal (base 10) number system, it becomes 65. This coding--a mark, five space signals, and a mark--always represents A and it always has a decimal value of 65 in the ASCII alphabet. The number value of an ASCII character, or a string of ASCII characters, is often used in programs or transmission systems for sorting or checking data.

Figure 2-1. RS-232-C transmission of one character. This string of pulses represents one ASCII coded character transmitted using RS-232-C signalling. The width of the pulses will change directly with the baud rate. The actual voltages used may vary from +3 to +4 volts for a space to -3 to -24 volts for a mark.

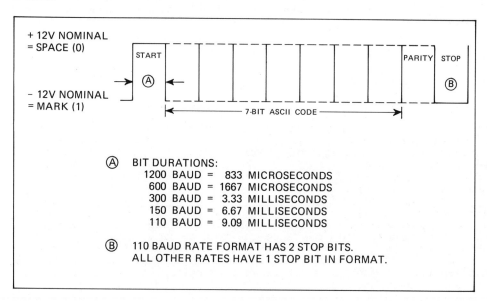

OTHER ALPHABET CODES

You may sometimes hear of other codes used for the transmission of
alphabetical characters. The simplest scheme, of course, is the
international Morse code. In Morse, as it is commonly called,
characters are represented by long and short pulses of light,
sound, or electricity, called dots and dashes. Morse is still
used in high frequency radio transmission, but it is often sent
and received by electronic terminals equipped with microprocessors.
    Baudot code is an older standard automatic printing machine
code which represents each character by five bits of data instead
of ASCII's eight. It is often referred to as a five-level code.
Machines using Baudot code are still common, and Baudot networks
serving deaf users are operating in many parts of the country.
The code shown in Table 2-2, however, was designed by Donald
Murray; it is quite different from Baudot's original five-bit code.
It is also known as the CCITT Alphabet Number 2. Note that there
are no real lower-case letters represented in the Baudot Code.

Table 2-2.   Baudot Character Alphabet

Code	Lower Case	Upper Case
Space 1 2 3 4 5		
1 1 0 0 0	A	-
1 0 0 1 1	B	?
0 1 1 1 0	C	:
1 0 0 1 0	D	$
1 0 0 0 0	E	3
1 0 1 1 0	F	'
0 1 0 1 1	G	&
0 0 1 0 1	H	British Pound
0 1 1 0 0	I	8
1 1 0 1 0	J	'
1 1 1 1 0	K	(
0 1 0 0 1	L	)
0 0 1 1 1	M	
0 0 1 1 0	N	.
0 0 0 1 1	O	9
0 1 1 0 1	P	0
1 1 1 0 1	Q	1
0 1 0 1 0	R	
1 0 1 0 0	S	Bell
0 0 0 0 1	T	5
1 1 1 0 0	U	7
0 1 1 1 1	V	;
1 1 0 0 1	W	2
1 0 1 1 1	X	/
1 0 1 0 1	Y	6
1 0 0 0 1	Z	"
1 1 1 1 1	LETTERS (Shift to Lower Case)	
1 1 0 1 1	FIGURES (Shift to Upper Case)	
0 0 1 0 0	SPACE	
0 0 0 1 0	CARRIAGE RETURN	
0 1 0 0 0	LINE FEED	
0 0 0 0 0	BLANK	

International Business Machines Corporation developed the Extended Binary Coded Decimal Interchange Code or EBCDIC. This eight-bit code is commonly used in connecting IBM equipment, particularly printing typewriters. Some software and hardware systems have been devised to allow communications between ASCII and EBCDIC speaking devices, but this is still not an easy task.

ASCII is the most commonly used coding system in micro-computer communications. Be wary of any equipment that does not speak this common language. Table 2-3 is not meant to be an exhaustive treatment of either the ASCII or the EBCDIC alphabet, but rather to show some of the differences and similarities be-tween these two common coding schemes. ASCII has more symbols and characters and can probably support non-English language symbols more easily. Both ASCII and EBCDIC contain unique codes used for transmission signaling, but they are not all the same.

Table 2-3. ASCII and EBCDIC Character Alphabets

ASCII Binary Code	EBCDIC Binary Code	Character
0 0 0 0 0 0 0	0 0 0 0 0 0 0 0	NUL
0 0 0 0 0 0 1	0 0 0 0 0 0 0 1	SOH
0 0 0 0 0 1 0	0 0 0 0 0 0 1 0	STX
0 0 0 0 0 1 1	0 0 0 0 0 0 1 1	ETX
0 0 0 0 1 0 0		EOT
0 0 0 0 1 0 1	0 0 1 0 1 1 0 1	ENQ
0 0 0 0 1 1 0		ACK
0 0 0 0 1 1 1		BEL
0 0 0 1 0 0 0		BS
0 0 0 1 0 0 1		HT
0 0 0 1 0 1 0		LF
0 0 0 1 0 1 1		VT
0 0 0 1 1 0 0	0 0 0 0 1 1 0 0	FF
0 0 0 1 1 0 1		CR
0 0 0 1 1 1 0		SO
0 0 0 1 1 1 1		SI
0 0 1 0 0 0 0		DLE
0 0 1 0 0 0 1		DC1
0 0 1 0 0 1 0		DC2
0 0 1 0 0 1 1		DC3
0 0 1 0 1 0 0		DC4
0 0 1 0 1 0 1		NAK
0 0 1 0 1 1 0	0 0 1 1 0 0 1 0	SYN
0 0 1 0 1 1 1	0 0 1 0 0 1 1 0	ETB
0 0 1 1 0 0 0		CAN
0 0 1 1 0 0 1	0 0 0 1 1 0 0 1	EM
0 0 1 1 0 0 1	0 0 1 1 1 1 1 1	SUB
0 0 1 1 0 1 1	0 0 0 1 0 1 1 1	ESC
0 0 1 1 1 0 0		FS
0 0 1 1 1 0 1		GS
0 0 1 1 1 1 0		RS
0 0 1 1 1 1 1		US
0 1 0 0 0 0 0	0 1 0 0 0 0 0 0	SP
0 1 0 0 0 0 1	0 1 0 1 1 0 1 0	!

ASCII Binary Code	EBCDIC Binary Code	Character
0 1 0 0 0 1 0	0 1 1 1 1 1 1 1	"
0 1 0 0 0 1 1		#
0 1 0 0 1 0 0	0 1 0 1 1 0 1 1	$
0 1 0 0 1 0 1	0 1 1 0 1 1 0 0	%
0 1 0 0 1 1 0	0 1 0 1 0 0 0 0	&
0 1 0 0 1 1 1	0 1 1 1 1 1 0 1	,
0 1 0 1 0 0 0	0 1 0 0 1 1 0 1	(
0 1 0 1 0 0 1	0 1 0 1 1 1 0 1	)
0 1 0 1 0 1 0		*
0 1 0 1 0 1 1	0 1 0 0 1 1 1 0	+
0 1 0 1 1 0 0	0 1 1 0 1 0 1 1	'
0 1 0 1 1 0 1	0 1 1 0 0 0 0 0	-
0 1 0 1 1 1 0	0 0 1 0 0 1 0 0	.
0 1 0 1 1 1 1	0 1 1 0 0 0 0 1	/
0 1 1 0 0 0 0	1 1 1 1 0 0 0 0	0
0 1 1 0 0 0 1	1 1 1 1 0 0 0 1	1
0 1 1 0 0 1 0	1 1 1 1 0 0 1 0	2
0 1 1 1 1 0 0	1 1 1 1 0 0 1 1	3
0 1 1 0 1 0 0	1 1 1 1 0 1 0 0	4
0 1 1 0 1 0 1	1 1 1 1 0 1 0 1	5
0 1 1 0 1 1 0	1 1 1 1 0 1 1 0	6
0 1 1 0 1 1 1	1 1 1 1 0 1 1 1	7
0 1 1 1 0 0 0	1 1 1 1 1 0 0 0	8
0 1 1 1 0 0 1	1 1 1 1 1 0 0 1	9
0 1 1 1 0 1 0	0 1 1 1 1 0 1 0	:
0 1 1 1 0 1 1	0 1 0 1 1 1 1 0	;
0 1 1 1 1 0 0	0 1 0 0 1 1 0 0	(Less than)
0 1 1 1 1 0 1	0 1 1 1 1 0 1 1	=
0 1 1 1 1 1 0	0 1 1 0 1 1 1 0	(More than)
0 1 1 1 1 1 1	0 1 1 0 1 1 1 1	?
1 0 0 0 0 0 0	0 1 1 1 1 1 0 0	@
1 0 0 0 0 0 1	1 1 0 0 0 0 0 1	A
1 0 0 0 0 1 0	1 1 0 0 0 0 1 0	B
1 0 0 0 0 1 1	1 1 0 0 0 0 1 1	C
1 0 0 0 1 0 0	1 1 0 0 0 1 0 0	D
1 0 0 0 1 0 1	1 1 0 0 0 1 0 1	E
1 0 0 0 1 1 0	1 1 0 0 0 1 1 0	F
1 0 0 0 1 1 1	1 1 0 0 0 1 1 1	G
1 0 0 1 0 0 0	1 1 0 0 1 0 0 0	H
1 0 0 1 0 0 1	1 1 0 0 1 0 0 1	I
1 0 0 1 0 1 0	1 1 0 1 0 0 0 1	J
1 0 0 1 0 1 1	1 1 0 1 0 0 1 0	K
1 0 0 1 1 0 0	1 1 0 1 0 0 1 1	L
1 0 0 1 1 0 1	1 1 0 1 0 1 0 0	M
1 0 0 1 1 1 0	1 1 0 1 0 1 0 1	N
1 0 0 1 1 1 1	1 1 0 1 0 1 1 0	O
1 0 1 0 0 0 0	1 1 0 1 1 0 0 0	P
1 0 1 0 0 0 1	1 1 0 1 1 0 0 0	Q
1 0 1 0 0 1 0	1 1 0 1 1 0 0 1	R
1 1 0 0 1 0 1	1 1 1 0 0 0 1 0	S
1 0 1 0 1 0 0	1 1 1 0 0 0 1 1	T
1 0 1 0 1 0 1	1 1 1 0 0 1 0 0	U
1 0 1 0 1 1 0	1 1 1 0 0 1 0 1	V
1 0 1 0 1 1 1	1 1 1 0 0 1 1 0	W

ASCII Binary Code	EBCDIC Binary Code	Character
1 0 1 1 0 0 0	1 1 1 0 0 1 1 1	X
1 0 1 1 0 0 1	1 1 0 1 1 0 0 0	Y
1 0 1 1 0 1 0	1 1 0 1 1 0 0 1	Z
1 0 1 1 0 1 1		[(left bracket)
1 0 1 1 1 0 0		/ (left slash)
1 0 1 1 1 0 1		] (right bracket)
1 0 1 1 1 1 0		∧ (caret or up arrow)
1 0 1 1 1 1 1	0 1 1 0 1 1 0 1	_____
1 1 0 0 0 0 0	0 1 1 1 1 1 0 1	'
1 1 0 0 0 0 1	1 0 0 0 0 0 0 1	a
1 1 0 0 0 1 0	1 0 0 0 0 0 1 0	b
1 1 0 0 0 1 1	1 0 0 0 0 0 1 1	c
1 1 0 0 1 0 0	1 0 0 0 0 1 0 0	d
1 1 0 0 1 0 1	1 0 0 0 0 1 0 1	e
1 1 0 0 1 1 0	1 0 0 0 0 1 1 0	f
1 1 0 0 1 1 1	1 0 0 0 0 1 1 1	g
1 1 0 1 0 0 0	1 0 0 0 1 0 0 0	h
1 1 0 1 0 0 1	1 0 0 0 1 0 0 1	i
1 1 0 1 0 1 0	1 0 0 1 0 0 0 1	j
1 1 0 1 0 1 1	1 0 0 1 0 0 1 0	k
1 1 0 1 1 0 0	1 0 0 1 0 0 1 1	l
1 1 0 1 1 0 1	1 0 0 1 0 1 0 0	m
1 1 0 1 1 1 0	1 0 0 1 0 1 0 1	n
1 1 0 1 1 1 1	1 0 0 1 0 1 1 0	o
1 1 1 0 0 0 0	1 0 0 1 0 1 1 1	p
1 1 1 0 0 0 1	1 0 0 1 1 0 0 0	q
1 1 1 0 0 1 1	1 0 0 1 1 0 0 1	r
1 1 1 0 0 1 1	1 0 1 0 0 0 1 0	s
1 1 1 0 1 0 0	1 0 1 0 0 0 1 1	t
1 1 1 0 1 0 1	1 0 1 0 0 1 0 0	u
1 1 1 0 1 1 0	1 0 1 0 0 1 0 1	v
1 1 1 0 1 1 1	1 0 1 0 0 1 1 0	w
1 1 1 1 0 0 0	1 0 1 0 0 1 1 1	x
1 1 1 1 0 0 1	1 0 1 0 1 0 0 0	y
1 1 1 1 0 1 0	1 0 1 0 1 0 0 1	z
1 1 1 1 0 1 1		{
1 1 1 1 1 0 0	0 1 1 0 1 0 1 0	¦
1 1 1 1 1 0 1		}
1 1 1 1 1 1 0		~
1 1 1 1 1 1 1		DEL

SOH: Start of Heading   STX: Start of Text
ETX: End of Text   EOT: End of Transmission
ENQ: Enquiry   ACK: Acknowledge
NAK: Negative Acknowledge   NUL: Null (non-printing fill)
HT: Horizontal Tab   VT: Vertical Tab
LF: Line Feed   FF: Form Feed
CR: Carriage Return*   BS: Back Space
DC1, DC2, DC3, DC4: Unspecified controls usually used "as
  needed" by manufacturers.

*Note that a carriage return moves the cursor or typing
head back to the first position in a line. It does not
move it down one line as is automatically done on a typewriter. A carriage return is usually accompanied by a line
feed to move the activity to the next line. Nulls are often
inserted to allow print heads the physical time needed to
perform a carriage return and line feed before the next
character is sent.

SYNCHRONOUS AND ASYNCHRONOUS TRANSMISSION

During the transmission of ASCII characters, we need some way to
tell when a character starts and stops. Two formats are used, one
called asynchronous and the other called synchronous. Both
formats require some additional information called framing bits to
be sent in order to tell when a character is starting or stopping.
The asynchronous format requires such framing information to be
sent with each character. Synchronous transmission gathers up
blocks of characters and only defines the beginning and end of
each block. Synchronous transmission is slightly faster and more
efficient than asynchronous, but it requires more precise timing
and is better suited to high speed transmission systems that
handle thousands of characters per second. Asynchronous transmission is the standard format used with microcomputer-based
systems.
    The asynchronous format adds a start bit to each character
that is to be transmitted. The start bit is a logical zero, or
space, and is represented by the positive voltage level on the
RS-232-C direct current line. The start bit tells the receiving
system to look at the next bits as an ASCII character. At the end
of the ASCII character, an eighth bit is added for what is termed
the parity check. This parity bit is a form of error detection
and correction, but it is seldom used in microcomputer communications systems. In sophisticated systems, the parity bit is
given a value (1 or 0) that will make the sum of the ones in the
eight-bit word come out to meet a predetermined standard--either
odd or even. This serves as a constant check on the quality of
the transmission. If the parity check is not the same value as
the value the transmitter and receiver have been programmed to
expect, various corrective actions could be taken. After the
seven bits of ASCII characters and the parity bit are sent, one or
more stop bits (logic 1) are transmitted. These stop bits insure
that the receiver recognizes the next start bit--and the whole
process starts over again, many times a second. The rate of
transmission determines how many stop bits are transmitted. Two
stop bits are usually used at lower speeds and one during faster
transmission. Transmission speeds for microcomputer systems are
usually designated as either 110 or 300 baud.

BITS AND BAUDS

Transmission speeds can be described in four ways. The particular description depends on what kind of work you are doing with a data communication system. The most common term used on electronic message systems and information utilities is <u>baud</u>. The baud rate is simply the measure of transmission speed. Baud rate is not the same as bits per second, and the two cannot be directly substituted for each other. It is like describing a stream of water. You can talk about the water moving at so many feet per second or you can talk about so many gallons passing a certain point in a second. They are two very different measures of the flowing stream. Baud rate is the equivalent of velocity. Mathematically, it is the reciprocal of the time duration of the shortest signal element in a transmission. This signal element in RS-232-C ASCII signaling is the time width of one RS-232-C bit. That time width for 300 baud works out to a little over 3.3 milliseconds. That means that each bit or voltage pulse is a little over 3.3 milliseconds in length. That is quick, but it is nothing compared to the state of the art in commercial circuits. Many circuits regularly operate at 1200, 2400, and 9600 baud.

  Bits per second is a measure of information transfer. It includes only information elements, not start/stop bits. The information element in our systems would be the seven-bit ASCII characters. This is a more practical measure of the information actually getting through a system. Bits per second is directly related to characters per second. Simple math tells us we need only divide bits per second by seven bits in an ASCII character to find characters per second. Another measure of information transfer is words per minute. Usually, a word consists of six letters (some formulas say five). Conversion from bits per second (BPS) to words per minute (WPM) would be done as follows:

$$\frac{BPS}{(7 \times 6)} \quad X\ 60 = WPM$$

This WPM figure is useful for persons trying to interface to printing terminals.

  The transfer of real information, separated from all of the framing and control information, is also referred to as <u>throughput</u>. Throughput can be measured in either bits per second, characters per second, or words per minute.

PARALLEL/SERIAL CONVERSION

A serial data communications channel is rather like a two-lane tunnel through a mountain which links two sections of a sixteen-lane highway. At each end, the traffic must funnel from eight lanes into one lane as it enters, and fan out again as it emerges at the other end. This process will limit the speed of the traffic in the tunnel, since as many as eight lanes of traffic must narrow down to one. The alternative is a sixteen-lane tunnel, which would, of course, be prohibitively expensive. Similarly, sixteen parallel wires (lanes) would be costly between two computers (or other devices) over long distances, so a two-wire serial method was devised to make possible cheap long distance data communications.

Before looking into the electrical device which makes this possible, we must stretch the tunnel example into a rather unreal scenario where all cars move in rows on the eight-lane highway in unevenly spaced clusters. As each cluster approaches the tunnel entrance, it must line up in single file. The car in the far right lane leads the way, with each successive car to the left queuing up behind the car which has been to its right. In the tunnel all cars travel at the same speed, and the spacing between cars in every cluster is the same. As the cars emerge from the tunnel, the first in line moves over to the far right lane; succeeding cars line up to the left of their predecessors and move on together down the eight-lane highway. Naturally, such a rigidly structured traffic pattern would be impossible to choreograph with cars, but it is essential for successful serial data transmission.

The electrical device which controls each "tunnel entrance" is actually a very capable "traffic cop." This device is often called a Universal Asynchronous Receiver/Transmitter--UART (pronounced YOU-art) for short. It is also called an Asynchronous Communications Interface Adapter, or ACIA. More recent versions are the Universal Synchronous/Asynchronous Receiver/Transmitters (USARTs), the Protocol Controllers, and an extraordinary development known simply as a Serial Input/Output (SIO) device. Regardless of what these devices are called, they all perform serial-to-parallel and parallel-to-serial conversions with minimal supervision by the host computer.

Because of the so-called intelligence of one of these devices, very little supervision is required. The very latest models, introduced to support the new sixteen-bit computers, are actually highly specialized programmable microprocessors in their own right.

Like our surrealistic highway and tunnel, a UART has two separate directions of traffic. The path that converts a parallel data output to a serial bitstream is called the transmit channel. The path that converts an incoming serial bitstream back into a parallel data input is called the receive channel. A very elaborate set of sensors and controls keeps the data traffic in precise syncopated rhythm.

The Western Digital TR1602 UART

To illustrate how a UART works, let us look at a real device: the Western Digital TR1602. From the outside it looks just like hundreds of other chips mounted in insect-like packages called DIPs (short for Dual Inline Package--they have two parallel in-line rows of pins). The TR1602 has forty pins, twenty in each row. As we describe what each pin does, remember that it is not very important to memorize the pin number for each function; you can always look up this information on the specification sheets if necessary.

There are three separate types of signals which are applied to the UART's pins: data, status, and control. Data signals in both serial and parallel form are manipulated within a UART and transformed from parallel-to-serial and back. Status signals indicate the progress of these transformations and signal any error conditions which occur. Control signals provide both internal and external sequence coordination. Since device power and ground voltages are supposed to be constant, they are not considered signals per se.

The TR1602 requires two power supply voltages: +5V and -12V. There is a pin for each of these voltages, plus a third one which is tied to ground. One of these (the +5V supply) is the main power pin. The other is used to provide a bias voltage, which is used inside the device as a sort of reference. Very little power is required for the bias supply, but it must be present. This extra power supply costs money, so most new successor devices to the TR1602 are designed to operate with just one power supply.

The transmitter side of the TR1602 has eight parallel trans-mit inputs (TR0-TR7) and one transmit data output (TRO). The conversion is done using a shift register, which is a formation of memory circuits that are loaded all at once (parallel) and emptied one at a time (serial). As each bit is transmitted out, those behind it shift into the memory circuits in front of themselves. The ripple effect gives the appearance of motion out of the device.

Because many internal operations are required to convert a parallel eight-bit input to a serial output, a transmit clock (TRC) pin is provided. This is not the computer system clock. There is no synchronization between the UART and the host, hence the term asynchronous. The frequency of the TRC signal sets the baud rate of the transmitted serial bitstream. The baud rate is the rate at which the serial 1s and 0s come out of the device. Many standard rates are used. For most serial transmissions over common telephone lines using standard Bell 103 compatible equip-ment, 300 baud is used. The TRC signal is almost always sixteen times the baud rate; for 300 baud the frequency of TRC is 4800 Hz (cycles per second).

Figure 2-2.   Telecommunication flow.

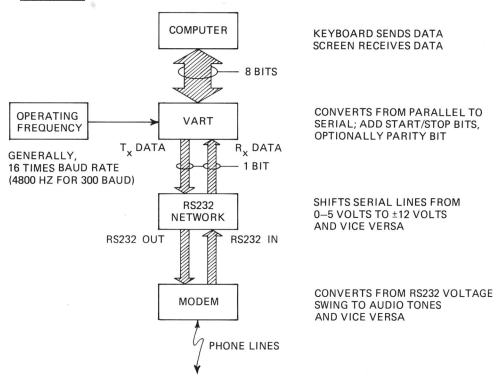

There is an inverse set of operations on the receive part of the chip, and the corresponding signals are <u>receive data input</u> (RI), <u>parallel data outputs</u> (RRO-RR7), and a <u>receive clock</u> (RRC) control signal.   Frequently, TRC and RRC come from the same oscillator, but this is not mandatory.   The two directions can operate independently at different baud rates, much as our tunnel could have a different speed limit in each direction.

There are two internal eight-bit parallel buffers that isolate the transmit-and-receive data holding registers from the computer system's data lines.   Two data strobe signals are used to initiate data transfers into and out of the holding registers at the appropriate times.   These control signals -- <u>transmit buffer load</u> (THRL*), and <u>parallel data read</u> (RRD)--are supplied by the host computer's serial device driver program.   When parallel data is output and latched onto the system's data lines, a strobe signal will immediately follow.   This is applied to the TR1602's THRL* line, opening up the internal lines which connect the transmit buffer (which has latched onto the data) and the transmit register.   The parallel-to-serial conversion circuits use the transmit register as their data source.   On the receive side, the RRD signal will open the connecting lines between the receive register and the parallel data receive buffer. This must be timed properly to avoid collisions on the system's data bus. There are three status signals which govern when these data strobes should be fired. When the transmitter section's parallel-to-serial process is complete, the <u>transmit register empty</u> (TRE) line goes to a logic 1. This is the signal that the host computer looks for before it sends more data and the THRL* strobe. When the data moves from the transmit buffer to the transmit register, the buffer is cleared, which sets the <u>transmit buffer empty</u> (THRE) line to a logic 1. THRE is used by the serial device driver routine to signal the arrival of data sent to the TR1602 upon receipt of the TRE signal, and it can be used to trigger the THRL* strobe.

Similarly, when the receiver section's serial-to-parallel process is complete, the TR1602 will output a logical 1 on the <u>data received</u> (DR) line. When ready to read this data, the host computer will output the RRD signal and read the data only when DR is 1. If parity is active, however, there is a safety status signal called <u>data received reset</u> (DRR*) which is set to a logic 0 if the parity-sensing circuits find an error and clear (set to zero) the receive register. The presence of this DRR* status signal will abort the data read operation if it cancels the effect of the DR status signal.

There are two control registers (one transmit, one receive) which are used to define the number of data and stop bits, and the use and sense (odd/even) of the parity bit. Each of these programmable features is set by control signals on the <u>word length select</u> (WLS1 and WLS2), <u>parity inhibit</u> (PI), <u>even parity enable</u> (EPE), and <u>stop bit select</u> (SBS) pins. The two word length select pins are used as a binary pair to set the word length to five (0,0), six (0,1), seven (1,0) or eight (1,1) bits. The parity function will be inhibited if a logic 1 is applied to the PI line. If parity is used, a logic 1 on the EPE line will generate even parity; a logic 0 will result in odd parity. Two stop bits will be generated with a logic 1 on the SBS line, unless a five-bit word length is selected, in which case a logic 1 will generate the standard 1.5 stop bits used by the five-bit Baudot code. A logic 0 on the SBS line will generate just one stop bit.

To prevent inadvertent redefinition of any of the control functions, the TR1602 will not accept any changes at its WLS1, WLS2, SBS, PI, or EPE pins unless the <u>control load</u> (CRL) pin is momentarily strobed to a logic 1.

Each cluster in the serial bitstream is distinguished from its neighbors by start and stop bits which frame it. Usually one start bit signals the beginning of a cluster and two stop bits identify its end. Sometimes a parity bit is included after the data bits and before the stop bits, when transmission errors must be detected before causing damage to later data.

There are usually eight data bits in a cluster. Fewer may be used if both the sender and the receiver permit it. In this form of transmission, the first and most basic requirement is that both ends expect the same number of data bits. The decision to use or to delete the parity bit follows in importance. Either one or two stop bits can be selected. One stop bit is usually used at 300 baud and higher, two stop bits at 110 baud.

Three status signals are generated upon the receipt of every cluster to guarantee that all three of the transmission parameters are properly set and that no undetected errors occur. These are: the overrun error (OE), the framing error (FE), and the parity error (PE). The first two signals are set to logic 1 levels only if an incorrect number of data bits are received, or an incorrect number of stop bits are received. Errors of this type, after communications have been established, are rare. The last status signal, the parity error, is set to a logic 1 only if the parity of the received data bit string (odd or even) does not match the parity bit. Parity, if used, can be preselected, either even or odd. If even parity is selected, the parity bit will be set to a logic 1 only when there are an even number of logic 1s in the data cluster. Conversely, odd parity would set the parity bit to 0 under the same conditions. Parity error signals are commonly used to trigger data retransmission. Because the parity bit (when selected) is found in every cluster, its use is often wasteful overhead.

If it is not used, the maximum length of each cluster is reduced from twelve to eleven bits--a 9% increase in the throughput of the link. This is such a significant benefit that parity is reserved for the very few applications where absolute accuracy is required (medical, nuclear control, and cryptological equipment, for example).

Continuous reading of the three status signals is not necessary. They are normally read at the beginning of each serial-to-parallel conversion cycle. A status flag disconnect (SFD) pin, held at logic 1, can be used to disable OE, FE, and PL signals. Then, by pulsing the SFD signals to a momentary logic 0, current samples of these three signals can be strobed to the appropriate sensing circuits. In this way, overall power consumption of the TR1602 can be reduced by cutting off current flow to pins when they are not being used.

Like most complex programmable digital devices, the TR1602 has a master reset (MR) pin. Its function is to reset (clear) both buffer registers. With the buffers empty, the TRE, THRE, and TRO signals will go to logic 1 levels automatically. It also resets the three error status indicators--OE, FE, and PL--plus the safety signal DRR*. This signal is generated by the host computer's software during device initialization.

The TR1602 description given here is an example of the functions of a typical device used in data communications systems. The data sheets for the UART, USART, or other device used in your system should be referred to for complete specifications before you attempt any hardware or software modifications.

WHAT THE FUTURE HOLDS

In this chapter, we have looked at the input/output ports of computers and terminals to understand how the digital data is coded and what kind of signaling is typically used. Once the data is out of the computer, it must be changed into a form that can travel over telephone lines if it is going to be used for long distance communications. The device that connects the computer to the telephone line--the modem--is the subject of Chapter 3.

chapter three

The Mighty Modem

All the data systems that communicate over telephone lines need a very important piece of equipment to link the telephone lines to the computer or terminal. This device is called a <u>modulator/demodulator</u> or <u>modem</u>. The modem modulates and demodulates audio tones transmitted over the telephone circuits. The telephone system of the 1980s is designed to carry only audio signals, in the form of alternating current voltages. Computers and terminals transmit information in and out, in the form of digitally coded direct current voltages. At some time in the future, all communications systems may be digital, and the telephone systems may accept direct current signals from homes and offices, but until that time, we must feed sound, not DC voltages, down the telephone lines. A modem sends and receives audio tones over the telephone line on one end, and direct current digital pulses for computers and terminals on the other end. The electronic components within the modem manufacture sound in response to digital voltage, and digital voltage in response to sound.

SIGNALING BY SOUND

The digital voltage signaling standard between the modem and the computer, or terminal, is normally based on the EIA standard RS-232-C. The frequencies of the tones used over the telephone lines are determined by another standard. The most common tone signaling standard in the United States is the one established by Bell Telephone Laboratories, called Bell 103. The Bell 103 standard is used for low speed modems operating up to 300 baud.

In digital communications, we are only interested in representing the digital 0s and 1s. We need to show those two states or conditions only. If we use sound to transmit digital information, we could simply turn the sound off and on to

Figure 3-1.   A modem and its functions.

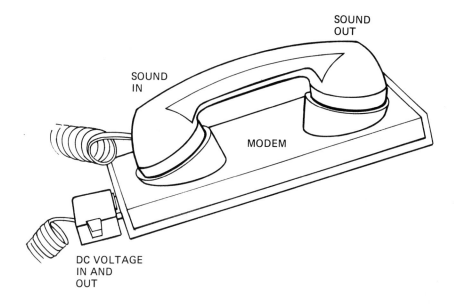

represent 0s and 1s, but this off-on signaling would leave room for error. The absence of sound might be a correct signal, but it might also be a broken connection or an interruption by noise. Two-tone signaling was adopted to represent digital information on audio systems. With two tones, we know that if tone A is not present, tone B should be. If neither tone is there, the system can immediately detect a problem.

   In the Bell 103 standard, the station that originates the

call (usually thought of as a <u>terminal</u>) uses a tone of 2225 Hz to represent a 1 and a 2025 Hz tone to represent a 0. Obviously, if the modem at the answering end transmits back with the same two tones, only one side of the conversation will be able to talk at a time. If, however, the answering equipment uses two different tones, we can use selective filters to detect only the desired signals, and a simultaneous two-way conversation can take place.

Simultaneous two-way transmissions over telephone lines is referred to as <u>full-duplex transmission</u>. Most modems (and all the low speed modems commonly used in electronic message systems) use four tones for signaling; two on the originate side and two on the answer side. The tones listed in Table 3-1 are those transmitted by each side. A modem transmits one set of tones, but it receives the other. Many kit builders and home designers have forgotten this and ended up only receiving their own tones.

Table 3-1: Bell 103 Standards

Type	Logic	RS-232 Voltage	Tone
Originate	1	-3 to -24 volts	2225/Hz
Originate	0	+3 to +24 volts	2025/Hz
Answer	1	-3 to -24 volts	1270/Hz
Answer	0	+3 to +24 volts	1070/Hz

Other modem standards, such as Bell 202, Bell 212, and the signaling schemes adopted by companies such as Anderson Jacobson and Racal-Vadic, are commonly found in commercial data communication systems. These modems use various schemes to provide higher signaling rates. The 202 series modems, for instance, are asynchronous devices that can transfer data at a maximum rate of 1200 BPS on standard telephone lines. But they only transmit in one direction at a time <u>(half-duplex transmission)</u>. They use a mark frequency of 1200 Hz and a space frequency of 2200 Hz. Complex <u>handshaking</u> signals are exchanged between the modems on each end of the line to control which modem will transmit at any given moment.

Some information and message systems can provide high speed transmission capability on an optional basis, but Bell 103 remains the standard for low speed data transmission in the United States.

ORIGINATE AND ANSWER

The majority of 103 type modems have the ability to switch between either originate or answer tone sets, but some do not. The originate tone pair will be used by almost everyone who uses a microcomputer as a data communications terminal. The only two instances where the ability to transmit answer tones is necessary are 1) when a computer is being used as an electronic message system and 2) when two computer users are communicating with each other directly. In the first case, users of the system will be transmitting the originate tone set and they expect to receive the answer tone set. In the second case, one of the operators must have a capability to transmit the answer tones in order to have a successful two-way simultaneous exchange. You might save some money by settling for an "originate only" modem, but be sure you will never need the answer capability. Most commercially available modems are now both originate and answer, but buyers should be particularly cautious when hunting for bargains. An "answer only" modem would only be useful for special purposes.

The actual coding of the characters sent out by a modem is the same as the coding of the digital stream going in. If the computer's digital signals are ASCII-coded, then the tones will also represent ASCII characters. The coding of the characters remains the same; a modem only changes the signaling method from electrical pulses to audio tones.

A TYPICAL MODEM: CAT

Let us take a look at the actual installation and operation of a very popular modem, the CAT, manufactured by Novation.

Figure 3-2. The CAT modem, manufactured by Novation, Inc., is a popular device marketed by several different companies.

The CAT is typical of many fine modems sold by Novation and other manufacturers; it serves as a good example of modem connection and operation. The CAT is sold under its own name and under the label of several other manufacturers. The CAT is compact and comes with its own power supply. It is ready to use when matched to a computer or terminal with the proper cable. The CAT provides all the standard features expected from a modern low speed modem.

Figure 3-3. The switches on the CAT
modem select between the originate and
answer modes and full-and half-duplex
operations. The RS-232-C cable and
power connections are also shown.
(Photo courtesy of Novation, Inc.)

It has a switchable originate-or-answer capability, a light-
emitting diode that indicates a received signal, and reliable
performance up to speeds of 300 baud. Included also is a self-
test capability that allows the modem to listen to itself for
testing purposes. This can be very handy when you are trying out
new equipment or software.

Direct Connection or Acoustic Coupling

The CAT comes in two versions: direct connection and acoustically
coupled. These terms refer to the way in which the modem marries
to the telephone. A direct connection modem actually plugs
directly into the telephone system at some point.

Figure 3-4. A more sophisticated
version of the CAT modem provides for
direct connection to the telephone line
and automatic answer capability.
(Photo courtesy of Novation, Inc.)

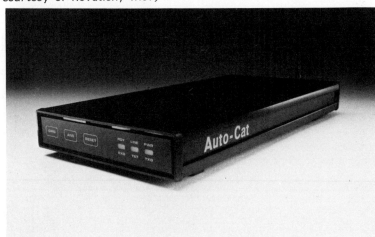

Some direct connection modems plug into a wall jack, and others are inserted between the telephone instrument and the handset. The direct connection version of the CAT is designed to be inserted between the telephone handset and the telephone body. The telephone is used in the usual manner, but when data communications are initiated, the handset is cut off and the modem electrically takes its place. This kind of connection means you must have a modern phone with the handset attached to the body by small modular plugs and jacks. In the United States, you can now obtain updated phones like these from local telephone companies or you can purchase them from many retailers.

The modern telephone system is sensitive to certain tones used by telephone control and signaling equipment. Direct connection to the telephone lines is allowed by the Federal Communications Commission only under certain conditions. Direct connection modems which plug directly into the wall must be certified to meet standards of tone purity and frequency. Uncertified equipment should never be directly connected to the telephone lines. Telephone companies can provide devices known as data access arrangements (DAA) to couple with uncertified equipment. Equipment connected on the handset side of the telephone instrument may not need certification, because the electrical network inside the telephone instrument provides the protection needed.

Figure 3-5. The MODEMPHONE by Racal-Vadic is a complete telephone and modem in one. The circuit board shown is installed in the MODEMPHONE. The DB-25 RS-232-C connector comes out the left side of the phone. Operation is controlled by the telephone cradle buttons and slide switch.

Figure 3-6. The Hayes Stack Smartmodem
is an "intelligent modem" containing its own
microprocessor and operating system. The
intelligent modem connects to a computer or
terminal through an RS-232-C port. It
receives the data to be transmitted and the
modem operating instructions over the same
data line. The modem's microprocessor
monitors the data stream for its own unique
command line. It has complete auto-answer
and auto-dial capabilities. All operating
parameters can be controlled from the
keyboard.

The Hayes Stack Smartmodem provides
unique flexibility because the computer
or terminal it is working with does not need
to have any interfacing software. The modem
is so "smart" that the terminal can be very
"dumb." This device sells for well under
$300 and accessories such as a clock console
are available.

The second way in which modems can be connected to the telephone lines is through acoustic coupling. In acoustic coupling,
the telephone handset is physically inserted into foam rubber
cups on the modem. Acoustic coupling has been used successfully
for many years and the acoustically coupled version of the CAT has
been popular and successful. But acoustic coupling has only one
advantage and several disadvantages.

The primary advantage of acoustic coupling is portability.
If you intend to travel with your system, an acoustic coupler will
provide the flexibility you need, as long as the places from which
you communicate have telephones with fairly standard handsets.
Modern streamlined telephones, some European phones, and replicas
of older phones will not fit into the cups on most acoustic
couplers.

The primary disadvantage of acoustic coupling is outside noise. Noise inserted into the telephone from nearby persons, airplanes, radios, or any other source can disrupt and actually disconnect data communications. Secondly, the mouthpiece of most telephone handsets is made from carbon granules which actually vibrate with sound waves and create electrical energy. When standard mouthpiece instruments are used for data transmissions over a period of many minutes, the carbon granules may "pack" or clump up and lose their activity. Tests have shown very large losses in efficiency after one hour's use. Packing takes place because the instrument is not being moved and because the constant repetition of the same two tones sets the granules into static patterns. Shaking or moving the handset can restore efficiency for a period of time. Finally, some harmonics can be generated because of the physical structure of the handset itself. These harmonics can be degrading to a signal trying to get through a weak or noisy connection. Novation and other dealers also sell dynamic or condenser microphone elements which acoustically coupled modem users can quickly insert into any standard handset. These elements are inexpensive, they do not pack or lose efficiency, and they limit harmonic distortion. They are very effective in increasing the reliability of acoustic modems. Novation calls their condenser type microphone, with electronic preamplifier, the Super Mike.

Figure 3-7. The Super Mike from Novation
replaces the mouthpiece in most telephones
and provides distortion-free transmission of
modem tones when using acoustically coupling
modems.

The DC Side of the Modem

So far, we have discussed the telephone end of a modem like the CAT. The end of the modem machine, which connects to the computer or terminal, is more complex and requires more attention to details.
    Some modems come with a cable already made for the system with which they will be used. ATARI and Radio Shack supply pre-wired cables for their computer systems. But even if you have a prewired cable, it is helpful to know what signals are passing over the wires. If you do not have a prewired cable, there are some things you must know in order to keep the 1s and 0s flowing in the right direction. The CAT uses standard RS-232-C wiring, so the following description applies to all standard modems.

What Signal Goes on What Wire

The connector normally used on RS-232-C cables is called a DB-25. A DB-25 has twenty-five pins and almost every one of them can be used for something in the RS-232-C signaling scheme. The wiring standard originally was designed to connect a terminal to a communications device. The pins are usually identified from the point of view of a terminal. However, in modern practice, some terminals are wired as communications devices because that is the role they serve.
    Many terminals have switch or wiring options. If you are connecting a modem to a terminal wired as communications device, the wiring standard can become very confusing. Remember, there are communications devices and there are data terminals. A computer is a data terminal, but a commercial terminal may be wired either as a data terminal or a communications device. It is really not as hard as it sounds. Let us look at an example.
    Although the connectors have twenty-five pins, the cable connecting a modem to a computer may have as few as three wires. One wire must be used to get data from the computer to the modem. Looking at the cable wiring guide, we can see this wire is connected to pin 3 of both cable plugs. Another wire has to be used to get data from the modem to the computer. This is

connected to pin 2. Finally, we need a common signal ground wire
to complete both direct current paths. This common ground is
always carried on pin 7. There is one other connection we may
have to make on the plug at the computer end. Since our transmissions are on a full-duplex circuit, we may have to defeat a
signaling option provided for half-duplex transmission.

Figure 3-8. DTE/DCE connections.

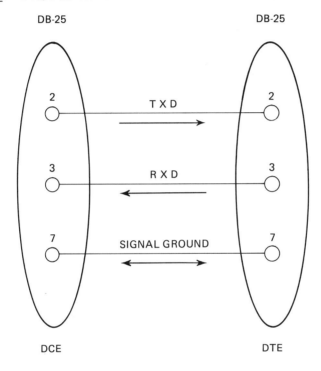

DB-25   DB-25

2   T X D   2

3   R X D   3

7   SIGNAL GROUND   7

DCE   DTE

DATA   DATA
COMMUNICATIONS   TERMINAL
EQUIPMENT   EQUIPMENT

(DATA SET/MODEM)   (TERMINAL/COMPUTER)

In half-duplex transmission, the devices on each end of the line pass signals called <u>request to send</u> (RTS) and <u>clear to send</u> (CTS) to coordinate their data burst. Since we use a Bell 103 full-duplex modem system, the RTS and CTS signals are not needed. The easiest way to by-pass this option is to route the computer's own clear signal back to its request line. This involves putting a short jumper between pins 4 and 5 of the DB-25 plug attached to the computer.

The wiring of a modem to a computer is simple compared to a modem attached to a terminal set up as a communications device. Both devices follow the communications equipment terminal wiring pattern. Both devices want to receive data on pin 3 and transmit it on pin 2. Obviously, hooking two transmits and two receives together results in no data transfer. Here again, we must fool the system. We have to transpose the wires in the cable so that pin 2 of each connector is attached to pin 3 at the other end. It seems obvious once it is explained, but many people have spent hours wondering why their modem will work with a computer acting as a terminal, but not with another terminal device.

Table 3-21.   RS-232-C Wiring Guide

Pin	Mnemonic	Function	RS-232-C Designation
1	GND	Protective ground. May tie together chassis so all equipment is at the same ground potential.	AA
2	TXD	Transmit data. Carries data from the modem to the computer.	BA
3	RXD	Receive data. Carries data from the computer to the modem.	BB
4	RTS	Request to Send. Controls the transmission on half-duplex circuits. RTS ON, +3 volts or more, tells a modem to transmit.	CA
5	CTS	Clear to send. Modem response to an RTS signal.	CB
6	DSR	Data set ready. Modem says it is on and ready.	CC
7	GND	Signal ground. <u>Must</u> be used.	AB
8	DCD	Carrier detect. Modem indicates it hears a tone.	CF

Pin Mnemonic	Function	RS-232-C Designation
9, 10	Used for special testing purposes.	
11	Not used.	
12	Secondary received line signal detector. May be used for a second, slow-speed circuit.	SCF
13	Secondary clear to send. May be used for a second, slow-speed circuit.	SCB
14	Secondary transmitted data. May be used for a second, slow-speed circuit.	SBA
15	Transmission signal element timing. For synchronous data transmission.	DB
16	Secondary received data. May be used for a second, slow-speed circuit.	SBB
17	Receiver signal timing. Used in synchronous data transmission.	DD
18	Not used.	
19	Secondary request to send. May be used for second circuit.	SCA
20 DTR	Data terminal ready. Computer tells auto-answer modem it can answer the phone.	CD
21	Signal quality detector. Used by special equipment.	CG
22	Ring indicator. Modem says the phone is ringing.	CE
23	Data signal rate selector. Not used in serial ports.	CH/CI
24 TXC	Transmit clock. Used in synchronous transmission.	DA
25	Not used.	--

The standard uses the phrases <u>data communications equipment</u> (DCE) and <u>data terminal equipment</u> (DTE). DCE obviously includes modems, but sometimes printing and video terminals are wired as DCE devices. DTE always includes computers, but sometimes terminals are wired as data terminal equipment. This can cause some confusion in how pins 2 and 3 are used. DCE is equipped with a female DB-25 connector. DTE usually has a male connector.

A control circuit is considered "on" when the voltage is more positive than +3 volts. It is "off" when the voltage is more negative than -3 volts.

Let us see what a typical operating session with a CAT modem is like. After properly connecting the cable between the modem and the terminal or computer we are using as a terminal, we need to check the power supply to the CAT. Most modems, and many computers, use the wall transformer/power supply combination to save space and heat in the computer cabinet. After the power supply is connected, moving the power switch to either "O" or "A" should cause the light-emitting diode on the top of the CAT to glow. Note that this three-position switch must be correctly placed in either "originate" or "answer" (probably "originate") when the power is turned on. Since the switches and connectors are often placed out of sight or toward the wall, you will have to learn the switch positions by feel. The other switch on the CAT chooses between full- and half-duplex and a special test mode.

Full- and Half-Duplex Modems

The term full-duplex (FDX) usually means that data can be sent and received simultaneously by a data communications device. In modems, that is exactly what the term means. The terms full- and half-duplex take on a slightly different meaning in reference to terminals, and we will discuss this shortly. First, let us figure out what to do with the "F" and "H" (full and half) switch on modems like the CAT.

With modems, full-duplex means simultaneous bidirectional communications using the two sets of modem tones described earlier. This is the most common form of operation for low speed data communications systems. Half-duplex means that the modem can only transmit in one direction at a time. This is similar to ham radio transmissions where each operator says "over" at the end of a transmission to signal the other that it is her turn. Half-duplex operation requires that the terminal and the computer control the modems through the "request to send" lead in the RS-232-C cable. Additionally, a modem operating in half-duplex will echo back a terminal or computer's own characters--a job usually done by the receiving end in a full-duplex operation. Half-duplex may be used in some unique situations, for example, where transmission in one direction is made at a slower speed because of the limitations of a printer on the line; but full-duplex is the standard mode of operation for modems used with information and message systems.

Full- and Half-Duplex Terminals
     The terms full-and half-duplex take on slightly different
meanings when they are associated with terminals or computers
acting as terminals. A terminal operating in half-duplex displays
its own characters on the screen (or printer) as they are transmitted. A terminal operating in full-duplex (or echo-plex, as it
is sometimes called) expects to have its transmitted characters
echoed back from the distant end (or from its own modem, if the
modem is in half-duplex.) In turn, it echoes back characters it
receives. A distant end echo serves as a positive and constant
check of the quality of the transmission path.

Figure 3-9. Full- and Half-Duplex Terminal.

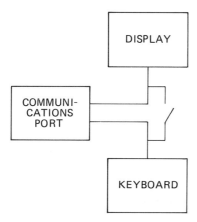

OPEN = FULL DUPLEX
CLOSE = HALF DUPLEX

If you are operating in full-duplex and you see garble coming up
on your screen, you know something is wrong in the signal path.
You cannot be sure if the problem is on the transmission from you
to the distant end, or from the distant end to you, but you can
be sure a problem exists.
     As handy as full-duplex transmission is to insure circuit
quality, it can also be a source of confusion to inexperienced
operators finding themselves with two or more characters on the
screen for every one they type. If your terminal is in half-
duplex and your modem is in half-duplex, your terminal will display a character as it is being sent and, again, as the modem
echoes it back. If the other end of the circuit is connected
and operating in the full-duplex mode, it too will echo the
character back and you will get three characters on your screen
every time you touch one key. This can be a real surprise,
particularly to a speedy touch typist. The product on the screen
is a jumble of characters and echoes of characters, but luckily
the cure is simple. Just read the simplex/duplex chart and set
up your system for the proper mode of operation. The full/half
switch on the CAT and similar modems should normally be left in

the "F" position, except when you are running a test in which you want a local echo of your own character transmissions.

Table 3-3.   Full/Half Duplex Settings

System A		System B	
Case 1			
Modem	Full-Duplex	Modem	Full-Duplex
Terminal	Full-Duplex	Terminal	Full-Duplex
Case 2			
Modem	Half-Duplex	Modem	Half-Duplex
Terminal	Full-Duplex	Terminal	Full-Duplex
Case 3			
Modem	Full-Duplex	Modem	Full-Duplex
Terminal	Half-Duplex	Terminal	Half-Duplex

In Table 3-3, only Case 1 will allow full echoing by both systems to provide a constant check on the quality of the circuit.   In Case 2, the modems each will echo back to their respective terminals.   This only provides a check of the local modem/terminal circuit.   The configuration in Case 3 is essentially no echo with the local display showing what was entered on the local keyboard.
    Any other switch or logic combination will result in either multiple characters or no characters being displayed.

Self-Test
The CAT provides a self-test feature which is a good way to try out terminal software and hardware operation before actually going on-line with a remote system.   The test mode is designed to check all portions of the modem's operation.   It does this by making its own transmit tones the same as the receive tones.   A telephone set must still be in place to feed the tones from the transmitter to the receiver.   The telephone must be free of any dial tones or ringing signals.   You can often achieve this for 30 seconds or so by simply dialing the first digit of your local exchange.   This test feature should provide you with a complete acoustically coupled check of your entire system.   It should echo everything you send.   A modem without the test feature can provide an echo check when you operate it in the half-duplex mode, but this does not verify the operation of the audio portions of the modem.
    After a successful self-test, you are ready to go on-line with a host system or a friend.   The combination of cabling, echo, and tone options may seem confusing at first, but they seldom change in operation and they become invisible when you begin to enjoy the world of data communications.

A modem like the CAT is a fine cost-effective device for most communications situations where a serial output is available from the computer. But often a serial output is an expensive option. Some modems are available which connect directly to the computer's main data path.

MODEMS FOR COMPUTERS WITHOUT A SERIAL PORT

Many popular computers, such as most models of the TRS-80, the Apple, and the ATARI, do not come with an RS-232-C serial port as a standard part of the machine. An extra I/O board, costing a hundred dollars or more, is necessary. This serial port is valuable for feeding both printers and modems, but often it would be nice to have a modem capability without the added cost of the RS-232-C interface board.

Several manufacturers have developed modem devices which plug directly into the main circuit board of the computer and interface the parallel data they find there with the serial outside world. These devices will be described in this book in association with the equipment for which they are designed. They include the Hayes Micromodem for the Apple II computer and S-100 systems, the LYNX for the TRS-80 and Apple II, and the Potomac Micro-Magic modem for S-100 bus systems. There is one series of modems which has models to fit several computers. These devices are known as the Microconnection and are manufactured by the Microperipheral Corporation in Redmond, Washington.

Microconnection devices are available for the TRS-80, the Apple, and the ATARI computers. The bus decoding version modem comes equipped with a cable that allows it to plug directly into the computer for which it is designed, without the use of a serial interface card or expansion module. Because of the unique interfacing, communications software with special address locations is necessary. The Microperipheral Corporation supplies appropriate software with each system. Additionally, several sources of communications software sell versions especially adapted for use with the Microconnection.

The bus decoding devices in the series have a unique capability: each bus decoding device not only interfaces with its appropriate computer and with the telephone line, but it also has an RS-232-C connector built in which can serve as a complete serial port in itself. The RS-232-C port can be used in several ways. It can be used to feed a printer which can print along with the data passing in or out of the modem in order to provide a permanent copy of data transmitted or received. It can be used as a separate RS-232-C connection for the computer without the modem/telephone portion of the system being activated. Finally, a Microconnection can serve as a standard RS-232-C modem without the use of the special interface to the computer system. The trade-off for this flexibility is the need for software to move the data in and out of the Microconnection.

Another significant feature is the provision for on-line data storage. The Microconnection is designed for easy electronic access to the modem tones being transmitted or received. A cassette recorder can be plugged into a Microconnection to record the on-line communications for later playback. This easy audio interconnection to the individual tones is also valuable for licensed amateur radio operators who may want to transmit and receive the modem's tones over radio links.

An advantage of some modem devices interfacing directly with the internal computer data stream is the ability to dial a telephone number automatically in response to commands from the keyboard or from software. Also, most of these devices provide an automatic answer capability which, combined with the right software, permit unattended remote access of the host computer.

These features are standard on some devices and optional on others. All directly interfacing modems are also direct connection modems; they do not use acoustic coupling. The Microconnection has another option for the use of European tone standards.

Modems which connect directly to the computer's data bus structure can provide a data communications capability at a reduced price. The decision to purchase the more traditional serial port/modem configuration or the bus-connected device depends a great deal on what equipment is already available and what special operating features you desire. Chapters 5, 6, and 7 will describe more options you may wish to explore. In the next chapter, we will look at more practical operational features. We will answer the following question: What is a terminal, and how do you tell if yours is dumb, smart, or brilliant?

chapter four

Terminals

Terminals are the doorways of a computer system. They let your data in and out. Without them, the world of data communications would be closed off to individual entry.

Terminals come in every size and shape. The cash register at your corner grocery store may be a terminal for a large inventory and billing system; people performing an inventory of the grocer's shelves may enter data into terminals that look like hand calculators. Microcomputers and minicomputers can serve as terminals for much larger computer systems. The devices that print airline tickets are actually "receive only" terminals. Most of us have seen video terminals in use at airports and municipal offices. Modern industry--including the travel and education industries--is becoming increasingly tied to computer terminals.

TERMINAL PARTS

Every terminal has three basic elements: an input device, a display device, and a communications port. The input device may be a full keyboard or a limited calculator-like keyboard; or it may be a device such as the light pen and the scanning wand now found in many stores. Paper tape and punch cards have long served to feed data into terminals equipped to read them.

Display devices include various kinds of printers, cathode ray tubes (CRT), flat-faced video screens called "plasma displays," and paper tape and cards. The graphic scoreboards found in sports arenas are actually the display devices of specialized computer systems. The terminal in your home, school, or office is smaller than the one in the stadium, but it could be just as spectacular.

The communications port on a terminal may use any of the signaling or alphabet schemes described in Chapters 2 and 3. The RS-232-C/ASCII configuration is the one most commonly used outside of IBM systems. Most video terminals have two RS-232-C ports. One port is used for communications and the other is used to drive a printer. In this way, a paper copy can be made of data that enters or leaves the video terminal.

PRINTING TERMINALS

There are several different types of terminals used in data communications systems. Originally, most terminals were teleprinters and automated typewriters. Many printing terminals are still in use.

Figure 4-1.   Printing terminals can be very convenient for many applications, particularly where extensive editing is not required. The Anderson Jacobson AJ 830 terminal and AJ 247 terminal and AJ 247 data coupler/modem make a practical and efficient work station. (Photo courtesy of Anderson Jacobson.)

These printers give a paper record of everything transmitted and received, and they have many important applications. Printing terminals may have some speed restrictions. The mechanical printing action may not follow the fastest communications circuits. Printing terminals can consume large quantities of paper and are usually noisy, but often there is no substitute for having a paper copy of the communications interchange. Until recently, printing terminals had a corner on the portable terminal market. The printing mechanism could be made much more portable than a CRT-based system. This has changed with the introduction of pocket sized terminals using liquid crystal displays. CRT systems form a separate branch of the terminal family called video terminals.

VIDEO TERMINALS

Video terminals are made by many different manufacturers and come with many different features and options. These options can be divided into three categories: screen options (including size, display, cursor control, and so on), keyboard options, and "intelligence." Intelligence is defined as the amount of electronic help built into the terminal device. If we can use the analogy of doors, a "dumb" door is one that you have to unlock, turn the knob, and open. A "smart" door is one that unlocks and opens in response to a button you press. A "brilliant" door recognizes you and, when you walk up to it, opens automatically. Terminals have similar capabilities: If you operate a microcomputer as a terminal, you may operate in either the "dumb", "smart," or "brilliant" modes. After we examine some standard terminal options, we will move on to the nuts and bolts of turning a microcomputer into a terminal device.

The screen options you choose in a terminal reflect how the display looks and what you can do with it. Some terminals can provide multicolor displays of graphic characters. Most provide a white-on-black screen display. Reverse video (black letters against white) and highlighting are common options. Simple charts or bar graphs can be displayed using standard characters to build the lines of the chart. Screen sizes range from a small five-inch diagonal to the more standard displays of about twelve to fourteen inches. Two important screen functions are formating and cursor control.

Formating refers to how blocks of letters and numbers are organized on the screen. Some terminals allow information to be displayed on split screens--like the pages of this book. Others provide status lines which are fixed lines of internal information about the transmission mode selected, characters sent and received, and other options selected.

The cursor on a terminal is a visual reference point. It usually shows where data will next be entered. Some cursors are simple blocks of light. Others are special symbols which change or blink off and on when certain options are selected. Many terminals can only enter data across the page and line by line-- just like a typewriter. Others allow their cursors to be "flown" around the screen so that data can be entered or corrected at any spot on the page. Cursors can often be moved by using directional keys and some units allow the cursor to be positioned on the screen by the use of numerical X and Y coordinates. Other cursor options include backspacing and an automatic "home" position at the top left corner of the screen.

Line width is an important variable. This is not related to physical screen size, but rather to the number of characters displayed in a line. Most standard terminals will allow up to eighty characters to be printed across in a line. (This is a carry-over from the eighty-column punch card.) Many will display only sixty-four characters, but this is standard letter width so it is perfectly acceptable for many activities. Most terminal screens allow for the display of at least twenty-four lines of data.

KEYBOARD OPTIONS

The keyboards found on video terminal devices may range from austere models with only about fifty keys to giants with over 100 keys and switches. The ASCII alphabet contains 128 characters and codes. A terminal keyboard that does not have the ability to transmit all those codes may be limited in some applications.
     Many computers will recognize only upper-case letters, so most terminals have a standard "upper case only" mode of operation available. However, when sending electronic mail, it is often preferable to use the common upper-case/lower-case mix. Many terminals feature a separate numeric pad for frequent entry of number data. Other special feature keys include: cursor control, tabulation, backspace, and screen formats (split screen, and so on). Many terminals include programmable special function keys. These keys perform certain specially defined functions when the terminal is running under the control of some kind of internal program. Possession of an internal operating program and internal memory puts a terminal into the "intelligent" category.

Figure 4-2.   The Hazeltine 1500 is a full capability terminal that has become a standard of
performance in the industry. (Photo courtesy
of the Hazeltine Corporation.)

INTELLIGENT, DUMB, SMART, AND BRILLIANT TERMINALS

"Intelligent," "dumb," "smart," "brilliant" --how can a terminal device be described by these words? A terminal can be classified according to how useful it is for performing a difficult or detailed job. The classification depends on the degree of programming and memory available within the terminal device.

A <u>dumb</u> terminal is no more than a keyboard, serial port, and display screen. The keyboard may be limited in the characters it can transmit. Often it cannot transmit lower-case characters or some control codes. The cursor simply marches along like a typewriter. It cannot be positioned on the screen. When data comes in, from the device on the other end of the communications link, it is printed out on the screen from top to bottom. When the screen is full, the text scrolls off the top and is lost.

During transmission, data to be transmitted must be typed in, a character at a time, while the terminal is connected to the distant device. All access codes, passwords, and other repetitive material must be typed in each time it is used.

Dumb terminals are sufficient for many uses and they are relatively inexpensive. They are often found in schools and in applications where neither operator nor computer time is at a premium. Adding some internal memory and programming to a terminal brings it into the <u>intelligent</u> class. The first step in the intelligence scale is <u>smart</u>. Different manufacturers define the terms to fit their equipment line. Let us look at one terminal that calls itself smart and see what features are provided.

The Lear Siegler ADM-42 is called a "powerful smart terminal" by its manufacturer.

<u>Figure 4-3</u> . The Hazeltine Modular One is a powerful terminal providing many operating conveniences. It has a graphics capability, full cursor control, detached keyboard, special function keys, pages of internal memory, and many other features. (Photo courtesy of the Hazeltine Corporation.)

Figure 4-4.   The Lear Siegler ADM-42, like
the Hazeltine Modular One, is a powerful
terminal. It, too, has a graphics capability,
full cursor control, detached keyboard,
special function keys, pages of internal
memory, and many other features. (Photo
courtesy of Lear Siegler, Inc.)

It has many of the screen and keyboard options discussed
earlier, including 1) the ability to display characters to attract
attention, 2) highlighting, 3) a fixed line showing the status of
the terminal, and 4) various editing commands. It has an internal
memory which can hold up to eight pages of text (2000 characters
per page). It has sixteen special function keys which can transmit
thirty-two prestored messages with one keystroke. These messages
can be as simple as one or two ASCII characters plus a carriage
return, or as long as sixty-three characters.

In operation, these features can provide increased efficiency
for both the operator and the computer. The operator can compose
up to eight pages of data (with the maximum ADM-42 memory option),
hold them in the terminal, and edit them until they are perfect.

Only then will contact be made with the computer so the pages can be transmitted efficiently at high speed. This method of composing data for entry saves on communications charges and computer time.

When entry is desired into the distant end or host computer system, the special function keys can automatically open the door. Computers usually require very specific log-on and entry sequences. Each step in the entry sequence can be accomplished by a preset special function key. Computer entry can be as simple as pushing keys 1,2,4,3. Similarly, many data and text entry functions require special commands. Programming these into the specially marked function keys ends the hunt for lost pieces of note paper and time-consuming reference to operating manuals.

When data is received from a distant or host system, the pages of memory available in most smart terminals allow the operator to review the material off-line, re-edit it, and then print it out on a printer attached to the second RS-232-C port. This ability saves operator time, computer time, and paper handling.

A brilliant terminal is actually only an extension of a smart terminal's capabilities. A brilliant terminal has more internal memory, external memory for long-term storage, and its own operating programs. In short, it is a fully equipped micro-computer.

The Perkin-Elmer 3500

If we took all the features and functions of a smart terminal and added a 6800 microprocessor, 48K of RAM, two disk drives, and an extensive package of utility and communications programs in read only memory (ROM), we would have a versatile communications machine. This description fits the Perkin-Elmer model 3500 Intelligent Terminal.

The 3500 is a microcomputer system optimized to perform as a terminal. It has an extensive disk operating system in ROM and comes with BASIC and assembly language programming features. As a terminal, it has every keyboard and screen feature imaginable. It can display selected characters at half-intensity, blinking, black on white, or underlined. It has special characters for business forms and provides movement of blocks, lines, and columns of data at the stroke of a key.

As each screen of information is developed, it is compressed and saved on disk by the operating system. The disk can provide long-term storage of all data transmitted and received by the terminal. The operating system provides all the software needed to process disk information locally or transmit it to another system or terminal.

Figure 4-5. The Perkin-Elmer 3500 Intelligent
Terminal is actually a stand-alone computer with
specially developed capabilities for operation as
a terminal. It can manipulate data in disk files
locally and exchange data with larger mainframe
systems. (Photo courtesy of Perkin-Elmer.)

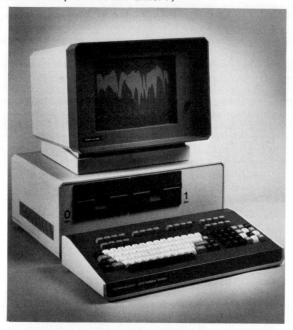

    Because this terminal can be programmed with detailed
instructions, it is capable of completely unattended operation.
Using an automatic dial modem, it can call a host system, sign on,
cue the host for the activity desired, transfer data, and
terminate the call--all without an operator. It can do this late
at night when communications costs are low and equipment is not
busy.
    The Perkin-Elmer 3500 evolved from a terminal into a micro-
computer specialized for data communications. It is possible to

approach the situation from the other way and specialize a standard microcomputer to act as a terminal. You may not get all the
sophisticated videos and features of the 3500, but you can develop
a brilliant and custom-tailored operating system.

PORTABLE TERMINALS

Before we leave our overview of dedicated terminal systems, we
should focus on the smallest members of the terminal family--the
portable terminals. Portable terminals help remove an obstacle
to communications that I call the "limitation of location." The
limitation of location used to mean that a data communications
user had to be physically near a rather bulky terminal device in
order to communicate. The hand-sized portable terminals now on
the market make it possible to duck into a telephone booth and
make a quick data call as easily as a voice call can be made.

Figure 4-6.   Portable terminals are becoming
much more important for the collection of data
away from traditional computer work station
locations. This utility worker is entering data
that will later be transferred to a mainframe
computer system for analysis. (Photo courtesy
of MSI Data Corporation.)

In 1967, MSI Data Corporation introduced a cart-mounted modified adding machine and tape recorder, powered by an automobile battery, that allowed a supermarket clerk to order products by entering data via the keyboard onto magnetic tape; the data was then transmitted to the warehouse over telephone lines. In contrast, the newest portable terminal weighs 22 ounces, is powered by four penlight batteries, contains a microprocessor and up to 64K of memory, and can be programmed for a wide variety of applications by the user. The MSI Omega Generation series of portable terminals are available with various programming and communications options. They are used in areas such as inventory, field service calls, utility meter reading, and manufacturing production lines.

Nixdorf markets a portable terminal called the LK-3000. This device began as a language translator, but it has been much more popular as a portable terminal. The LK-3000 is programmed with plug-in modules. The modules allow the system also to serve as a calculator, notepad, or translator.

Figure 4-7. The NIXDORF LK-3000 portable terminal can provide on-line or stored modes of operation. (Photo courtesy of NIXDORF.)

In operation, some allowances must be made for the keyboard and display size of any portable terminal. Typically, the keys have several functions they each can perform. Operators must learn specific shift functions to get the most out of each keystroke. Numbers can be entered quickly, but typing letters is slow until skill is gained through practice. These units display only a single short line at a time, but data can be stored and replayed line by line if needed. Dedicated host systems can easily be programmed to transmit data line by line when working with portable terminals. A separate modem device is needed to communicate over telephone lines. An acoustically coupled or direct connection modem can be used.

The most common function for a portable terminal is data collection in the field. After the data is collected, it is held and later dumped to the host system directly or by telephone. The limitation of location has been severely decreased, if not destroyed.

A very sophisticated portable terminal device such as the MSI 88f is capable of all the program options found on any larger intelligent terminal, including prestored log-on and transmission prompts. This hand-held terminal is limited in size only by the need to make the display and keyboard easy to use.

Figure 4-8. The MSI Data Corporation 88f is a programmable portable terminal able to provide a handful of sophisticated operations. (Photo courtesy of MSI Data Corporation.)

In the next chapters, we will look at practical ways in which available microcomputer systems can be made to serve as data communications devices.

chapter five

Using the Apple II Microcomputer as a Data Terminal

We have reviewed much of the technical and theoretical background of data communication systems. It should be clear that if you want to participate in the world of data exchange, you need two things: a terminal to transmit and display data, and a modem to send the data over telephone lines. A microcomputer can serve as a very effective terminal; it only needs the right program and modem combination. This chapter will deal with methods of making a very popular microcomputer--the Apple II--into an efficient and effective data terminal.

THE APPLE

The Apple II computer is manufactured by Apple Computer Company of Cupertino, California. It uses a 6502 microprocessor as a central processing unit (CPU) and has a full line of accessories available, including disk drives, joysticks, and sophisticated systems to control lights and appliances remotely. Many companies sell accessories and software for this microcomputer system. A survey of several thousand data communicators showed that over 24% use Apple II computers as terminals. If you do not own an Apple computer, this chapter can still serve to demonstrate how easy it is to set up a complete brilliant data communication system.
     There are several decisions to be made in configuring your Apple as a terminal. Some of the decisions are based on what equipment you already have and what operating capabilities you want to obtain. Essentially, you must add two new items to your computer: a modem and software.

MODEMS FOR THE APPLE

The Apple is popular, so there are several modems available. A standard Apple II does not come with an RS-232-C serial port. Special circuit boards, often called communications cards, are available from several manufacturers--including, of course, Apple Computer Company--to provide an RS-232-C data port. A serial communications card plugs into one of the accessory slots in the Apple and directly interfaces with the data bus. The card effectively becomes a part of the computer and the RS-232-C signaling provides the interface to devices outside the cabinet.

If you already have such a card--perhaps to interface with a printer--then your modem decision may be driven by economics. You can shop around and find the best price on any RS-232-C Bell 103 standard modem and interface with it through the communications port of your Apple II.

Apple Computer Company has two interface cards capable of providing RS-232-C signaling. The simplest is called the Serial Interface Card. A more complex device is called the Communications Interface Card. According to Apple Computer Company the Serial Interface Card is "intended for applications that use data rates other than those handled by the Communications Interface Card (110 or 300 baud), or that involve serial printers that don't require 'handshake'." In the case of the Apple II microcomputer, you should not attempt to use the Serial Interface Card for data communications purposes. They make a special Communications Interface Card for that purpose.

The Communications Interface Card has software in ROM on the card which allows easy interface with programs written in BASIC. It comes with an operating manual which describes operating and interfacing techniques.

If you do not have a serial card of any kind, or if you want special software-controlled operating features, you still have several modem makers from which to choose. The first company to market a modem on a circuit card which plugs directly into the Apple was D.C. Hayes Associates. Their firm has since changed its name to Hayes Microcomputer Products. Under either name, their Micromodem II is a compact circuit board containing a complete parallel/serial conversion system, modem, and some internal firmware.

Figure 5-1. The Micromodem II consists of a circuit card that plugs into the Apple II microcomputer and a telephone coupler. It comes complete with all cables and integrating software in ROM. (Photo courtesy of Hayes Microcomputer products, Inc.)

The output of the modem is fed to a <u>data access arrangement</u> (DAA) supplied with the unit which interfaces with the telephone line. There is no RS-232-C output available, only the connection into the telephone system. Direct connection allows the modem system to answer a ringing telephone line and to dial outgoing calls.

The Micromodem II plugs into one of the Apple's accessory sockets. The circuit board has a 1K ROM containing a program that allows operation of the Apple II as a dumb terminal--with some special features. This dumb terminal can dial a telephone number as it is entered into the keyboard. A small relay on the circuit card pulses the telephone line just like a dial. This will work even in areas using dual tone multifrequency (push-button) dialing systems. The Micromodem II can also answer the phone when it rings and communicate in several different modes of operation.

The operating program contained in the ROM can be called with a few keystrokes. It resides quietly until called. The dumb terminal portion of the program allows you to transmit, receive, and display data. No data is saved in memory. When it scrolls off the screen, it is gone. The program is efficient and convenient. The program and all its options are controlled directly from the keyboard. The system can dial a number, hang up, and change baud rates upon keyboard command. When the Micromodem II Program in ROM is called, all other programs running on the system are frozen. They can be resumed immediately after you are done communicating.

When the Micromodem is active, the program constantly checks to see if a ring signal is coming in from the telephone line. An operating option called <u>remote console</u> automatically answers the phone if it rings and allows the calling party to operate the Apple II remotely. This is very handy, for instance, for persons who would like to operate their home system from terminals at work or school. Remember, though, the serial data system has no practical graphics capability. You cannot play a game using graphics by remote control because the graphic characters rely on a very special kind of video mapped display. The remote console option turns the Apple II into a practical time-sharing system, but it will not play games using graphics over the telephone line.

The Micromodem II program can be called by a command in a BASIC program. This means that the real power of the system is as great as the programming you read into it. In practice, complete BASIC language bookkeeping systems could run through their data unattended and then place a phone call and transmit the final account data files. After the call is completed, the BASIC program could be resumed with no loss of variables. Very complex and sophisticated communications programs can be written to weave the Micromodem II into the Apple II to make an extremely powerful terminal system. We will see just such a program shortly.

NOVATION'S APPLE-CAT II

But the Micromodem II has competition. Novation has a version of the CAT modem called the Apple-Cat II.

Figure 5-2. Apple-CAT II is a highly sophisticated
integrated modem system with many options.

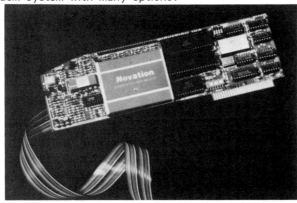

It is physically very different from the standard CAT in that it
is a single circuit card which plugs into the Apple II's accessory
socket.   It provides automatic dialing, answer and disconnect
functions, plus operation at 300 or 1200 baud.   This 1200 baud
feature is unusual in a modem of this type and price (about $400,
including software).
     In the 1200 baud mode, the Apple-Cat II uses the Bell 202
signaling technique (1200 Hz mark, 2200 Hz space, half-duplex
transmission with various clear and request-to-send signals being
exchanged). Most message systems do not have a Bell 202 signaling
capability, so this mode would most commonly be used under special
arrangements with another Apple-Cat owner. Many business and research systems use 202 signaling with their remote terminals
operating under a polling system.   In this kind of service, a
remote system "dumps" data when it is periodically polled by the
central computer. The 202 signaling scheme is provided in the
Apple-Cat because it is technically easy to do with the same high
technology large scale integration devices used to make the 300
baud tones.   The 202 standard is widely used by amateur radio
operators transmitting on the very high frequency bands.
     The 1200 baud systems can spoil you very quickly. The 400%
increase in speed produces a screen of data in a few seconds.   If
you then go back to the 300 baud mode, the characters seem to
crawl along each line.
     The software needed to operate the Apple-Cat II is supplied
on disk, so this device is best suited for use with systems
equipped with disk drives.   The program is menu-driven and very
easy to use.   It provides complete support for the auto-dial and
auto-answer functions and can save and transmit data in disk files.
     The Apple-Cat II is a unique and flexible modem device.
Various options are available including tone decoders, Murray/
Baudot operation for the deaf, and software that allows wireless
remote control of external devices. An external telephone handset may be connected to the unit so it can serve as a complete
telephone system. The Apple-Cat II/Apple II combination provides
one of the most powerful and flexible data communications systems
available today.

ASCII EXPRESS II: A BRILLIANT COMMUNICATIONS PROGRAM

Simple modem devices can be used along with the Apple II to give it an elementary communications capability, but more extensive operating features are provided by special software packages. One of the top pieces of communications software for the Apple II computer is the ASCII Express II, written by Bill Blue and marketed by Southwestern Data Systems. This program works with the Micromodem II to provide a brilliant terminal capability for the Apple II.

Figure 5-3. The ASCII Express smart terminal program for the Apple II provides many fine operating features. After the sign-on shown here, the program presents several command menus for easy selection of options.

The ASCII Express II is a complete disk-based package of programs which allows you to quickly and easily transmit and receive disk files of any type (binary files must be converted to ASCII). The program requires at least one disk drive, 48K of RAM, and either the floating point ROM or a language card to operate. It also interfaces with various lower-case adapters such as the card marketed by Dan Paymar. The program disk includes a versatile line-oriented editor, as well as an index system to keep track of the telephone numbers of systems you call frequently. It includes special keyboard "macro" functions designed to allow you to sign on to called systems semiautomatically. Let us see how the system works.

The first thing you should do with any new program you receive is to read the instruction manual. The manual for the ASCII Express II contains thirty pages of valuable information in a high quality format. Both step-by-step instructions and more descriptive discussions are included in the manual.

The second thing you should always do with a new piece of software on disk is to back it up, that is, make working copies of the disk for daily use. The ASCII Express has a copy program right on the disk. You need this copy program because it is the only one that will successfully reproduce the ASCII Express program. Copies can only be made from the original master disk; the "cloned" disks cannot be reproduced by normal means. The master disk will allow only four copies to be made. These four copies are enough for anyone's normal use; the limitation on making copies is a very effective way to stop the problem of boot-legging programs. Users should be careful, however, to read the instructions fully so they do not waste any of the available copy passes with procedural errors. The copy program on the disk can be used an unlimited number of times to copy any other disk, so it is a valuable disk operating utility by itself.

After the program is copied and personalized to your system according to the instruction manual, you can put it "on the air." There are three major portions of the operating system: the macro file, the terminal program, and the line editor.

The Macro File
The macro file system provides one of the very convenient operating features of this program. Each macro is a large piece of information that can be transmitted by a two-key sequence. The information can include any sign-on codes or passwords and commands to be transmitted to move the remote system to whatever function you want to perform. When you select one of the eighteen prestored telephone numbers from a menu, the proper macro commands for that system are loaded automatically. Up to twelve macro commands can be associated with each telephone number. Each macro is transmitted by a dual key-stroke of two specially designated keys.

If a Hayes Micromodem II or a Novation Apple-Cat II is in the system, the computer will dial the number (it will even show you each number on the screen as it is dialed). If an integrated auto-dial modem is not available, you will have to do the dialing; the computer will show you the number and do the rest.

You have to manually load each macro file into the system the first time, of course. But after that, operation is nearly auto-matic. The macros can be used for more than just signing on. Any series of commands regularly sent out can be loaded into macro files. This feature saves reference to operating manuals and notes penned on the back of envelopes. Any experienced user of data communication systems will appreciate the value of this ASCII Express II feature.

The Buffer
The buffer is an important part of this program. The buffer is a workspace in RAM. It can be filled with received data, data from disk files, or characters typed from the keyboard. It can be added to or cleared. It can be dumped to named disk files, viewed on the screen, or transmitted out the modem port. The buffer is the scratchpad for data communications. It is the workbench where you work on data with the program tools provided on the disk. A 20K buffer is provided by the ASCII Express II. This is enough to hold about ten minutes of continuous character transmission at 300 baud.

The Terminal Program

Many different transmission features are under program control. Half- and full-duplex transmission options can be selected from the keyboard. The baud rate can also be changed on command. The Apple II, running under the ASCII Express II, will transmit 126 ASCII characters by using a combination of keys.

The terminal mode of the program is the major program tool. This mode is the one in which the actual work of communications is done. In this mode everything typed on the keyboard will go out the modem port, and received data will be displayed on the screen. (Note, of course, that data echoed from a host computer will also be displayed.) The buffer can be used to save all displayed data for later storage in disk files, or the data can be sent out to a printer after editing. A printer, connected to the Apple II through its own interface, can print along with the screen so instant hard copy can be obtained. (The printer must be capable of a speed of at least thirty characters per second.)

A separate option is available to allow a disk file to be loaded into the buffer and transmitted to a host system. This option provides for systems like CompuServe's EMAIL and some other message systems which send a prompt when they have digested one line and are ready to receive another. The program will look for a specified prompt before sending the next line or character of data.

Another subroutine allows receipt of files from a host system. In this mode, you can receive data in a "formal" or "informal" manner. The informal manner simply feeds all incoming (or echoed) data into its buffer. The formal mode issues a particular command to the host (for example, MAIL READ) to tell the host what data to send and then enters the receive mode. This technique lets you capture the information you requested with no other dialogue between you and the host being retained in the buffer.

The Line Editor

The third major portion of the ASCII Express II program package is a line editor which allows you to work on data in the buffer and change, add, or delete characters on a line-by-line basis. This is useful for cleaning up received files prior to printing and for preparing messages to be saved for later transmission to a host system. This kind of off-line message preparation saves long distance telephone bills and system use charges and allows you to transmit error-free and concise messages. It is not as easy to use as a character-oriented word processing program, but as an accessory to a communications program it is first rate.

Other utility programs on the disk allow entry into and conversion of various kinds of disk files for data transmission.

The ASCII Express II is the final ingredient needed to turn the Apple II microcomputer into a powerful communications terminal. But there are other popular microcomputers and other combinations of hardware and software available. The following chapters deal with those systems and combinations.

chapter six

Using the TRS-80 as a Terminal

The Radio Shack TRS-80 line of computers, particularly the system now called the Model I, has become the most popular microcomputer system in the world. My survey of thousands of information utility users showed that 31.5% were using TRS-80s to communicate. The Radio Shack line of systems is extensive, and the number of options and combinations of accessories from many manufacturers is large. This chapter will concentrate on untangling the world of data communications options for the TRS-80 Model I and Model III computer systems. The Model II and Color Computers have very simple and efficient communications capabilities which are easy to use and explain. Let us begin with the most complex of the TRS-80 computers, the Model I.

THE MODEL I

The TRS-80 Model I is no longer manufactured, due to increased regulation on the amount of radio frequency interference microcomputers may emit. However, with well over 250,000 units previously sold, this system will be important for years to come to anyone interested in microcomputers.

An understanding of the components of the TRS-80 Model I system will later help you understand the uses of alternative pieces of equipment. The keyboard section houses the actual computer CPU, ROMs for the operating system and the BASIC language, and up to 16K of memory. Various connectors on the back of the keyboard bring in power, the cassette I/O port, and the expansion bus. The expansion bus on a TRS-80 Model I is extended through a forty-pin connector and cable. The system enclosed in the keyboard housing is the fundamental building block of the TRS-80. It is a stand-alone computer capable of loading and saving programs from cassette, and running complex BASIC programs in the RAM space available. Many manufacturers have provided options to add to the system from this point, but let us see how it was originally designed for expansion.

The Expansion Interface for the TRS-80 Model I provides room to house extra RAM, a controller chip for the disk system, a real time clock, a printer output, a second cassette, and a serial card to provide an RS-232-C I/O port.

Figure 6-1. The Expansion Interface for the
Radio Shack TRS-80 Model I holds optional
memory, disk controller, clock, and RS-232-C
serial interface devices. (Photo courtesy of
Radio Shack.)

Under the standard configuration, it is necessary to have the
Expansion Interface and serial card to use the TRS-80 as a terminal. Radio Shack originally marketed a separate RS-232-C/Bell
103 modem which was the Novation CAT wearing a Radio Shack label.
Their most recent modem is an in-house development called Modem I
which operates in a standard fashion, but which also has a capability to interface to the keyboard computer system without the
Expansion Interface. A special cable and program is needed and
only half-duplex operation is possible without the Expansion
Interface. Radio Shack also has Vidtex cassette-based programs
for data communications.

All these pieces together allow the system to communicate.
But the Expansion Interface was an expensive option and some
individuals who were happy with 16K and cassette storage objected
to buying the Expansion Interface simply to be able to add the
serial data card.

Figure 6-2. The Serial Interface card translates
between the parallel expansion interface bus and
RS-232-C serial data. It can only be used in the
expansion interface. The slide switch on the card
determines if the DB-25 connector is wired as a
terminal or as a computer. The DIP switch is
used to select transmission parameters. (Photo
courtesy of Radio Shack.)

Similarly, the RS-232-C serial data card was an extra cost and many users wished to integrate a modem device directly into the computer bus. Of course, other users were not happy with the Radio Shack software and wanted a smarter software package. The industry responded with a flood of telecommunications hardware, software, and integrated packages.

HARDWARE

There are many ways to make the TRS-80 Model I into a data communications terminal.

Figure 6-3. This picture shows the variety of hardware that can be used to turn the TRS-80 Model I into a communications terminal. These devices include the D-CAT modem, LYNX, Micro-connection, TERMCOM, and the Expansion Interface. Each device represents a slightly different approach to the problem of providing a communications capability for the TRS-80 Model I.

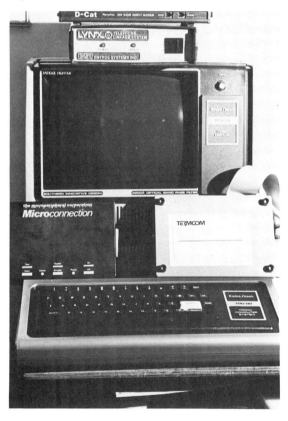

Let us start at the telephone end of the system and look at the
options as we go along.

The Radio Shack/CAT modem worked well but, as originally
marketed, it was an acoustically coupled device. Many users
substituted direct connection devices, such as the D-CAT, and
gained the advantages of direct connection. The newer Modem I is
a direct connection device.

Figure 6-4.   Modem I from Radio Shack is a
complete RS-232-C modem with both direct
connection and originate/answer capabilities.
With optional software and cable it will interface with the TRS-80 Model I without the use
of the Expansion Module. In this optional mode
it will only provide half-duplex service. As an
RS-232-C modem it will work with any computer
or terminal and provide full operating options.
(Photo courtesy of Radio Shack.)

The Radio Shack serial card uses an RS-232-C standard DB-25 connector, so any RS-232-C/Bell 103 modem will work with it.

The Expansion Interface is the biggest target of alternative communications devices. The double cost of the serial card and the Expansion Interface led to competition from other devices.

Figure 6-5. These three devices each replace the parallel/serial I/O function of the Expansion Interface. LYNX is a complete modem, TERMCOM provides an RS-232-C port, Microconnection provides both a modem and RS-232-C I/O service.

One approach to the replacement of the Expansion Interface was taken by the Statcom Corporation. Statcom markets a device called TERMCOM, described as an intelligent interface box. TERMCOM comes complete with connectors and cables to mate with the TRS-80 keyboard computer package. TERMCOM takes its power from the computer power supply and mates with the computer data bus.

The TERMCOM interface provides an RS-232-C port. This unit is a useful option if you already have a modem or you want RS-232-C signaling for some other purpose, but you do not want to invest in the Expansion Interface and serial card. The heart of the unit is a universal synchronous/asynchronous receiver/transmitter (USART) which translates between the parallel signals on the TRS-80 data bus and the serial format. The device has switches for selecting data transfer rates and formats. Jumpers on the circuit board control the number of stop bits and other options. TERMCOM can be used to interface with any standard modem or printer using RS-232-C signaling.

Figure 6-6.   The TERMCOM device borrows power
from the TRS-80 and interconnects the parallel
bus to RS-232-C devices. The connectors at the
top are for the RS-232-C and power cords.

An integral part of the total TERMCOM package is the software. The software can be ordered for systems from a 16K level
II to a 48K disk system. The TERMCOM software provides a very
advanced terminal capability. Let us look at a slightly different solution to the TRS-80 data communications puzzle.

LYNX

EMTROL Systems manufactures controllers and processors for
industry. They have entered the microcomputer market in the
area they believe has the best potential for growth: data
communications. They market a modem and serial interface called
the LYNX.

Figure 6-7. LYNX modem.

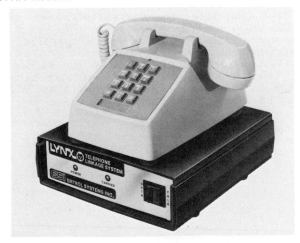

The LYNX provides a complete direct connect modem capability for the TRS-80 Model I without the need for the Expansion Interface and serial card.

LYNX uses telephone modular plugs and jacks (type RJ11) to connect directly to the telephone system. It plugs in series between the wall socket and the telephone. When the LYNX is in use, the phone is disconnected. If your telephone is not equipped with modular jacks, you may have to ask your local telephone company how to make the connection. Many electronic supply stores and telephone stores have adapters to connect the modular jacks to the older style square four-pin system. They may be provided at no charge from some telephone companies. Cables with a modular jack at one end and spade lugs on the other are also available. The LYNX is certified by the Federal Communications Commission (FCC) for direct connection into the telephone system.

The other connections on the LYNX are for the power supply and the data bus. LYNX uses the same data ports as the Radio Shack RS-232-C serial card, so the serial card cannot be in the system at the same time. Any standard TRS-80 Model I software package will work with the LYNX.

The LYNX is simple to use. A back panel switch selects the originate or answer mode.

Figure 6-8. The back of the LYNX modem device has connectors for the telephone line and power cord and switches that set trans- mission parameters and originate/answer options.

The front panel has one big switch labeled "Talk" and "Data." Two light-emitting diodes show if AC power is on and if a carrier has been detected by the modem's receiver. Parity, number of stop bits, and transmission mode are set by internal switches, but the software can override these settings by keyboard command.

The LYNX also comes with its own software package on cassette, but any program designed to run with the standard TRS-80 data configuration will run with the LYNX. One version of the LYNX EMTERM program designed for the elementary and inexpensive TRS-80 Level I system (4K of memory and Level I BASIC). This means that a complete terminal system can be put together using only the simplest TRS-80 Level I, the LYNX, and the simple version of the EMTERM program. This combination gives good capability at a low price. LYNX sells in the $300 price range.

The only major capability missing from such a system is the ability to drive a serial printer to capture on paper the information that marches by on the screen. The next system we will review provides that capability.

THE MICROCONNECTION

Versions of the Microconnection can be used with many micro-computer systems.

Figure 6-9. The Microconnection can connect to either the keyboard computer or the Expansion Interface. It provides full modem, audio, and RS-232-C interfaces.

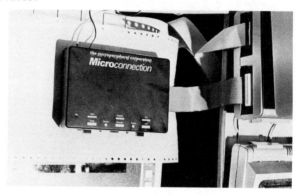

It will be described here in conjunction with the TRS-80, but variations of the Microconnection exist for the Apple II, the PET, and the ATARI computers. An RS-232-C version is also available.

The Microconnection is manufactured by the Microperipheral Corporation in the state of Washington. It can probably best be viewed as a kind of magic "black box." The bus decoding version is a three-way translator. If you put audio modem tones into it, both RS-232-C signals and parallel eight-bit bus-addressed signals come out. Similarly, RS-232-C signals come out as audio tones and parallel data. The parallel data port is tailored for the micro-computer system with which it is to be operated.

The audio portion of the Microconnection is a direct connection FCC-certified modem; it also uses the modular RJ11 plugs. The Microconnection plugs into the telephone circuit in parallel with the telephone by using a "Y" or duplex modular jack. This is available from the Microperipheral Corporation or Radio Shack (Radio Shack part #279-357). This type of connection allows the telephone to be used as a monitor and local testing device. Additionally, the audio lines in and out of the modem are available on separate jacks. This unique feature allows audio recording and transmission of the ASCII tones from a recorder and it provides a handy interface for amateur radio operators who want to use a modem on the VHF ham bands.

The audio recordings of modem tones can be stored and played back later for printout or transfer to another system. Programs and data can be played back through the modem ports of micro-computer systems that have very different cassette or disk systems. High quality recorders with speed accuracy must be used for this purpose, but audio recording gives a practical alternative to disk file systems for storage of material, too. The modem need not be connected to the telephone line for use of the recording or playback feature.

The Microconnection RS-232-C port uses a standard DB-25 fe-male connector. This connector is wired as Data Terminal Equip-ment (DTE). It transmits data out of the Microconnection on pin 2 of the DB-25 and receives it on pin 3. If you want a paper copy of the data received in the modem port you only have to attach an RS-232-C printer to the DB-25 connector. This same port can be used to drive the printer for more traditional uses without the modem being hooked to the phone lines.

When used with the TRS-80 Model I, the Microconnection plugs directly into the expansion port on the keyboard computer module or the screen printer port on the expansion interface. The Microconnection has an auto-answer auto-dial option.

In operation, the Microconnection offers great simplicity and flexibility. The basic unit has three switches. One switch puts the device into the telephone circuit. The second selects between originate and answer operating modes and the third switch turns the power off and on.

Figure 6-10. This interior view of the Microconnection shows the DB-25 connector and audio
jacks at the top, various function switches at
the bottom, and the parallel interface cable on
the right. The telephone line is attached to
the screw posts at the left.

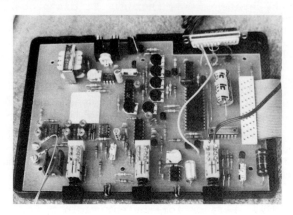

     The instruction manual for the Microconnection is superb. It
describes methods of using the telephone for local tests, special
telephone situations, audio recording, amateur radio operation,
troubleshooting, and much more. The instructions are detailed,
yet very easy to follow. The instruction manual also provides
details on the S80 terminal program supplied with each unit.
     The S80 terminal program provides simple terminal operation.
It comes on a cassette and will work with any TRS-80 Model I, even
the Level I 4K system. The bus decoding version of the Microconnection uses a port address which is different from the
standard TRS-80 configuration. This means that software for this
system must use port 208 for data and 209 for status messages
and it must meet the Microconnection protocol. Several dealers
have software packages optionally configured for the Microconnection, but standard software will not work with this device.
An advantage of this kind of addressing is that a sophisticated
user can retain the original addressing with an Expansion Interface (or LYNX or TERMCOM), use the Microconnection at the new
address, and have two independent or interconnected serial ports.
     The Microconnection line of communications devices is avail-
able with many options. The auto-answer provision permits unattended remote access of the host computer. A detector is
provided for ring counting and preset answer conditions. Auto-
dial comes with the auto-answer version. Another option allows

the Microconnection to be used with European standard modem tones. Versions of the Microconnection for TRS-80, ATARI, PET, and Apple computers sell for about $250; various options are extra.   An RS-232-C only version (actually a standard modem) sells for under $200.

So far we have described four different hardware combinations which will provide a communications capability for the TRS-80 Model I.   The systems vary in price and capability.   Each user can have the fun of designing an individual system based on available equipment and needed capabilities.   A major part of every data communications system is the software and there is a great deal of communications on the market.

TRS-80 MODEL I SOFTWARE

Many different kinds of software are available to make the TRS-80 Model I into a communications terminal.   The programs vary in the complexity of the hardware required to operate them, the degree of intelligence, and the price.   One problem all software designers encounter is the Model I's limited keyboard and ASCII character generation capability.   The TRS-80 Model I does not come equipped to deal with control codes or lower-case characters easily.   Most information utilities and message systems operate more efficiently if control codes are used.   Various software designers have met the keyboard limitation in different ways.   Some simply ignore control codes and leave the user to work around situations where their use would speed service.   Others have redefined or redesignated certain keys to produce control codes under certain conditions.   Each of the programs available provides its own combination of requirements, flexibility, and cost.

EMTERM

The EMTERM program that comes with the LYNX is a good program to examine first.   It loads in from a cassette and can be transferred to disk.   It does not have an extensive file handling capability. It provides for the transmission of control characters and has several additional features.   It is economical and practical.   It comes with the LYNX at no added cost and will work with the TRS-80 Level I.

EMTERM, like most communications programs, is menu-driven. A menu of alternatives is presented on the screen and the desired alternative is chosen by entrance of a number or letter.   The main menu provides alternatives:

STORE MESSAGE	(S)	
RECEIVE BASIC	(R)	(Level II systems only)
TRANSMIT BASIC	(X)	(Level II systems only)
TERMINAL	(T)	
VIEW/CHANGE UART	(V)	
BASIC	(B)	

The "STORE MESSAGE" feature allows preparation and storage of a message off-line for later transmission. Message storage is done in a 1K buffer allocated by the program. This feature allows the user to save valuable on-line time because the message goes out much faster than the average individual can type.

The "RECEIVE BASIC" option for the Level II system allows the receipt of a program written in BASIC from the distant system. EMTERM contains a special relocation feature which tucks the communications program away in high memory and leaves the normal RAM work space free. The received program is saved in the RAM work space and then can be RUN, LISTed, or CSAVEd. This program transfer is best accomplished with another system running EMTERM and using the TRANSMIT BASIC mode.

The "TERMINAL" option provides the normal conversational mode of operation. In this mode, all data received is lost when it scrolls off the screen, and all data sent must be entered on the keyboard. It is possible to toggle on and off a printer connected to the parallel port of the TRS-80 to allow simultaneous printing of the displayed characters.

Some system diagnostics are presented by this program. If a mismatch of either parity or word length (the framing bits) occurs, diagnostic letters appear on the screen. This is a unique program feature, but often the framing errors detected are not serious enough to interfere with character transmission.

The parity, word length, and number of stop bits can all be decided from the keyboard. These entries temporarily override the switch settings on the LYNX circuit board.

The EMTERM program provides a message buffer and BASIC program transfer capability; it also can provide for the transmission of control codes including "BREAK" and "ESCAPE." An output buffer also is provided to accommodate slow parallel printers.

Program startup is simple. After setting memory size and loading EMTERM, entering "SYSTEM" brings the question "New starting address?" on the screen. If you follow the guidelines in the instruction manual, and you answer with a four-digit hex relocation address, you send EMTERM off to high protected RAM or any chosen block of memory. After EMTERM is stored in protected RAM, BASIC programs can be loaded and run normally (except that a small portion of memory is not available). The BASIC command "SYSTEM" "/" (relocation address in decimal) will restore the EMTERM menu without affecting the BASIC program.

In practice, EMTERM is a practical program for use with various information utilities such as the Source and CompuServe. The S80 program provided by the Microperipheral Corporation with the Microconnection provides most of the same capabilities.

S80

S80 is also a cassette-based program designed to run with the simplest hardware. The S80 program uses the "up" arrow to shift into the control code mode. The number keys can also be redefined to provide some of the brackets and other symbols sometimes used by large systems, but which are not available on the TRS-80 Model I keyboard. The action of a printer can be controlled through the parallel port. There is no off-line message preparation or simple program exchange capability.

While these two programs come free when you purchase the equipment, they are fairly representative of about ten elementary communications programs available for the TRS-80 Model I. They provide a good basic communications ablility, but each has its own limitations. Data communications users quickly find they want more powerful programs, and there are several good ones available.

SMART PROGRAMS

There are certain functions and attributes a good smart commu- nications program should have. The list of necessary items includes:

1. Excellent documentation including all operating informa- tion and details on customizing programs. A good program must have a good operating manual.
2. The ability to prepare files off-line for later trans- mission. If messages and programs can be read in and automatically transmitted, a great deal of money can be saved in long distance telephone calls and system use.
3. Buffer storage that can be turned off and on. The ability to quickly open and close the buffer allows a kind of rough preediting of the data to be saved. It saves time and paper during later printing.
4. Prompted transmission of lines or characters from the buffer. Some systems prompt for transmitted data. If a communications program will not wait for and recognize the prompts, a great deal of data can be lost.
5. The ability to transmit frequently needed strings of characters (MACROs) with the touch of a key. These macros greatly simplify signing-on and using systems.
6. Complete support of all control characters and, if possible, lower-case characters too.
7. Ability to transfer files stored in a format other than ASCII. (These files are converted to ASCII before or during transmission.)
8. Some degree of screen formatting. For example, words do not break in the middle if the transmitted line is longer than the display screen.)
9. Control over an auxiliary printer.

There are several programs which come close to meeting the standards listed, but at least three match it perfectly and add some frills of their own.

SMART 80

The SMART 80 series of programs is written by Dick Balcom and marketed by the Microperipheral Corporation which produces the Microconnection. Several different versions of the program are available to support different equipment combinations.
Since one version of the Microconnection is designed for use without the Expansion Interface (which holds the disk controller), a SMART 80 program is available on cassette. It loads files to and from the cassette almost as easily as other

programs do with a disk. It is by far the most powerful cassette-
based communications program available for any microcomputer
system.

Another SMART 80 version works with Stringy Floppy (TM) high
speed tape system manufactured by Exatron. This combination gives
a low cost alternative to disk drive storage. The only thing a
disk drive system can do better is make frequent entries into a
data file. Frequent file access is very uncommon in terminal
operation.

Of course, a very powerful disk version of SMART 80 is
available which is compatible with all major TRS-80 Model I
disk operating systems, including double density.

SMART 80 adds some features to the above list of "must have"
items, including an automatic upload and download of files from
CompuServe and Forum 80 systems and between users, transmission
of assembly language files, and speed selection which slows the
throughput of characters to insure that the receiving system
receives all the data, even if it is heavily loaded and running
slowly. Two prestored messages (macros) of up to thirty characters are available. The keyboard is provided with an automatic
repeat key function, and a "beep" tone is sent out the cassette
port each time a key is depressed. A speaker connected to the
cassette port will provide positive feedback on each keystroke.
This greatly improves the "feel" of the keyboard system--especially
for typists who are used to mechanical systems where something
goes "bang" each time a key is depressed.

The SMART 80 software costs between $80 and $100 in the
various versions. It is available in versions addressing either
the Microconnection or the standard TRS-80 operating ports.

ST80
Another available series of programs, written by Lance Micklus,
is called ST80. The series includes low cost communications
software, but it is capped off by a fine program called ST80-III.
ST80-III also fits the definition of smart terminal software given
above. It provides for one prestored sign-on message of up to
sixty-three characters. A unique feature of this program is the
option for encrypted transmission. Files can be moved into RAM,
converted to ASCII if they are not already converted, and
scrambled by a random number generator driven by a twenty-five-
character password. They can then be saved again for later transmission. The scrambled files can only be unlocked by someone
using the ST80-III program who knows the password. This feature
may be particularly useful where industrial security or personal
privacy is important.

ST80-III features a set of software translation tables which
work on all transmitted and received data. The translation tables
allow detailed customizing of the software, so it can communicate
with practically any system including large mainframes. Some
large system manufacturers make unique use of control codes during
data transmission. ST80-III can be instructed to translate codes
so they have meaning to both systems, or so the TRS-80 ignores the
codes it does not need. As an example, some mainframe systems
send control codes for data formatting which are used by modern
printers for controlling the type size. A printer copying along
with the data input might strangely if these commands are passed

along exactly as received. The ST80-III translation table allows a tremendous degree of flexibility and sophistication to be programmed into the TRS-80 Model I.

ST80-III includes a feature called Veriprompt (TM) which checks echoed characters against transmitted ones. This feature insures accurate transmission of data. The characters are checked "on the fly." The system does not send one character and wait for the echo, but rather looks back to compare transmitted characters with echoed ones while still sending new characters. At most, two characters are in the system at a time.

ST80-III has many other operating features, including the ability to execute any of the disk operating system commands directly from the program. This allows great flexibility in operating and file manipulation.

This software for the Model I sells for about $150 on disk.

OMNITERM

OMNITERM is a program written and distributed by David Lindbergh. OMNITERM also uses a translation table system, but it is more extensive than the system found in other software. It is specially designed to use both ASCII and other codes such as EBCDIC with equal ease. OMNITERM also features the ability to see text that has scrolled off the top of the screen, and the ability to fully reformat the screen so that 80, 40, 32, or any other column width will appear neatly as sixty-four-column text on the TRS-80 screen.

The features of OMNITERM will please the most sophisticated users. It has many special transmission commands which make it particularly useful for persons who check into several different kinds of systems. The screen formatting capability and scrolling of data greatly aid in the use of electronic mail systems. Many message systems send thirty-two-column lines because of the display size limitations found in some microcomputer systems operating as terminals. A TRS-80 Model I, II, or III does not have this display size limitation. OMNITERM will change the carriage returns in these short lines to a space. It will fill a line as full as possible and insert its own carriage return when the next space character is found. This prevents the fragmented lines found in most "wrap around" programs and provides the user with full clean lines of text.

Screen formatting produces messages that look better and are easier to read; scrolling allows quick recall of message specifics. This is particularly useful when writing an on-line reply to an electronic mail message. If you can quickly look back to the message you just received, you can pick up details important to the reply you are composing. This look-back feature circumvents one of the great disadvantages of electronic mail (as it is presently formatted) over paper mail. Electronic mail usually requires you to compose a reply without direct reference to the note to which you are replying. A paper note is usually available for reference while you compose the reply.

OMNITERM is a sophisticated program, but it is easy to use because--like all the smart terminal programs described here--it is menu-driven. OMNITERM sells for about $100 on disk.

HARDWARE AND UTILITIES

Most of these intelligent terminal programs require at least 32K
of RAM to operate. (Some SMART 80 programs can run in 16K, but
you will have a small buffer.) They can operate with the various
modem systems described above, but special versions are required
for the Microconnection. They all come with some utility programs
that perform various functions. The most common utility is one
that allows the creation and the saving of off-line messages.
Other utilities may change files to ASCII or compress files for
more economical transmission. A TRS-80 Model I using any of
these programs will become one of the most powerful data communications devices available today.

MODEL II, MODEL III, AND COLOR COMPUTERS

What about the rest of the TRS-80 line? All the large systems
have a data communications capability. The Model II and Color
Computers come with an RS-232-C port as a standard part of the
equipment. The Model III needs only an RS-232-C card as an extra
cost hardware option (it is provided with the dual disk 32K
package). The systems need a standard modem to interconnect with
the telephone line.
   Communications software for the Model II comes on the
standard operating system disk. It is a menu-driven program; it
provides buffer storage, file capability, and keyboard change of
transmission parameters. The ST80-III terminal program is also
available for the TRS-80 Model II.
   The Color Computer has a special Radio Shack Videotext program which provides a terminal capability specially configured
for the CompuServe information utility. The ability to prepare
locally messages off-line for later efficient on-line transmission
is provided. The program allows the transmission of control codes
and it recognizes the cursor positioning and screen formatting
commands (to clear screen, and so on) sent by CompuServe. Upper-
and lower-case characters can be transmitted. The Color Computer
running the Videotex communications software can be used to
communicate with any message or information utility. The program
on a cassette plus one hour of CompuServe computer time are
available from Radio Shack stores for about $30.
   The TRS-80 Model III is not directly compatible with Model I
communications software. The Model III routes data differently
internally, and assembly language programs must be changed to
support this system. The disk format is also different. A Radio
Shack Videotex communications package, similar to the one
described above for the Color Computer (but without off-line
message preparation) is available for the Model III on cassette.
The program will load and run on either the Model I or Model III
and it is very easy to transfer from cassette to disk.
   The SMART 80 program is also available in a version that
provides smart terminal operation for the TRS-80 Model III. It
provides all the standard SMART 80 features plus complete cursor
control. Smart 80 is available for the Model III on both disk
and cassette.
   Versions of ST80-III and OMNITERM are also available for the
Model III with the complete features of those programs.

chapter seven

S-100 Bus Computer Systems and CP/M

A certain extended family of computers is defined by the way the systems connect internally. These are the computers using the S-100 bus. This bus structure is a physical and electrical configuration that describes the size and shape of printed circuit boards, the characteristics of various voltages and signals, and the pins that make particular power or data connections. It is the electrical and physical path the signals and power voltages take. The bus structure allows computers to be changed or expanded in a modular fashion. In theory, a standardized bus allows circuit boards made by several different manufacturers to work together in the same computer. In practice, this is not always the case.

The S-100 bus originally was developed (its detractors claim it was not "designed") to be used with the 8080 microprocessor. It is called the S-100 partially because it has 100 parallel circuit paths. The faster and more powerful Z-80 microprocessor can be used on S-100 bus systems, but it does not fit perfectly because of the added signal lines the Z-80 can use. Similarly, CPU circuit boards using the 6800 microprocessor have been adapted to S-100 systems. The S-100 bus is not a perfect standard. S-100 systems are often troubled with cross talk between signal lines and parasitic oscillation. Manufacturers often customized the standard to suit their own design--a practice which created frustration among computer owners trying to integrate a system. The Institute of Electronic and Electrical Engineers (IEEE) has released standard 696 for S-100 bus structure which should reduce problems with incompatibility. Many products are now on the market which advertise their compatibility with the IEEE standard.

The S-100 bus was originally introduced by MITS on its Altair computer in 1976. It was also used by IMSAI at about the same time. Neither of those companies is active at this time, but the S-100 bus has become an industry standard simply because of the market it created in memory and peripheral devices.

CURRENT SYSTEMS

There are several modern commercial champions of the S-100 bus structure. (It is indicative of this industry's growth that

systems sold in 1976 can be considered "antique" less than a
decade later.) North Star, Polymorphic Systems, and Dynabyte all
market complete S-100 bus systems. Companies such as SD Sales,
Morrow, Jade, and Integrand make components for S-100 systems.
One of the most popular S-100-based computer systems is the
North Star Horizon.

Figure 7-1. The North Star Horizon microcomputer is a complete well-integrated system
using the S-100 bus. It is equipped with two
serial ports: one usually used for a terminal and
the other for other peripherals such as a modem.
The Horizon can run under the powerful North Star
Disk Operating System or CP/M.

The Horizon computer is a complete integrated package, with
the flexibility and expandibility of the S-100 bus. The disk
drives and controller are normally internal to the unit, as is
the power supply. In keeping with this design philosophy, the
Horizon comes with two integral RS-232-C serial ports. One port
is used to interface with a terminal using local DC signal
connections. The other port can be used for a printer or modem.

A good library of software is available for North Star disk
drive systems. Most other S-100-based disk drives do not have a
large quantity of software available "off the shelf." Until late
1980, a data communications program for North Star systems, called
Telestar, was marketed by Leonard E. Garcia. Mr. Garcia dis-
continued marketing the software for personal reasons, but if
you are a North Star user you might find a copy of Telestar available through local computer stores or software dealers--it is still
in wide use.

A sophisticated terminal program called CROSSTALK is available for North Star from the Microstuf Company. CROSSTALK runs under the North Star disk operating system. Received and transmitted data can be saved in a buffer and the buffer contents can be transferred to disk files. CROSSTALK will be described in more detail later in this chapter. The Telestar and CROSSTALK program packages are useful to North Star users, but what about the users of other S-100 bus systems?

THE SOFTWARE PROBLEM

Software simply is not "portable" between the various disk systems available for use on the S-100 bus if the unique operating systems are retained. Certainly 8080 assembly language programs (like Telestar) have some universal applications among the 8080/Z-80 kinds of equipment, but the disk drive, I/O port, and file handling routines are quite unique even among S-100 systems. A great deal of customizing is required to assure that a program designed for the North Star will run on a Polymorphic Systems computer, even though both computers have the same bus structure, and the CPUs recognize the same assembly code programs.

UNIVERSAL SOFTWARE INTERFACE

The lack of portable programs has led to the popularity of a de facto standard operating system for 8080/Z-80 systems called CP/M. CP/M is an operating system designed by Digital Research and "CP/M" is their registered trademark. Just as the S-100/IEEE 696 bus has become a standard for hardware connection, CP/M has become the software interface standard or the software "bus" (though not an IEEE standard). CP/M is not unique to S-100 bus computers. Many microcomputers built on a single board or with other interconnect structures can and do operate under CP/M.

CP/M is an operating system. The operating system is the most fundamental level of software. It is always on-line during normal operation and most of the time it is "transparent" or at least "opaque" to the user. It is the first level of software to talk to the user. When you first tell your computer to load a language (BASIC), you are probably talking to the operating system.

The exact definition of the operating system may differ for various kinds of equipment. Most microcomputers have some sort of monitor (usually in ROM) looking for keyboard inputs and other signals. Many disk systems load a disk operating system in from the disk which integrates with the monitor and forms the operating system. Operating systems may be contained totally in ROM, or they may be read in totally from tape or disk after the system is "booted" alive with a wired or switched-in startup routine. An operating system provides the software routines to move data in and out, put it on the disk, and interface with higher level languages.

In theory, if everyone used the CP/M operating system, identical higher level languages and programs could be loaded into all machines. This does not, however, imply total disk portability. There are some factors, such as physical disk size

(5¼- vs. 8-inch) and format (density), which prohibit the transfer of a disk from one CP/M machine to another. The so-called big disk (8-inch) single-sided single density systems offer the best opportunity for interchangeability. A CP/M disk made in this format can be carried to most other 8-inch CP/M systems and run with no problem. This is not true of most 5¼ disk systems running under CP/M. The same programs can be run on all systems if they can be entered in, but getting the programs in may still require a specific disk format for the disk hardware in use.

Once the CP/M operating system is customized to the hardware it is on, the details of the hardware (aside from the disk differences) become almost irrelevant. It presents a universal face to the outside world, while internally performing routines needed to run the specific machine. A program need only be designed to run with CP/M, not with any particular microcomputer or disk system.

Several microcomputer manufacturers have developed operating systems which use the CP/M standards for software interface. Cromemco, for instance, has a disk operating system called CDOS, which is not CP/M, but it will respond to CP/M commands and interface with CP/M programs.

CP/M consists of a monitor control program plus some utility programs. The disk includes utility programs such as a text editor, an assembler, and a debugger. This total package enables the user to create, edit, debug, assemble, and run programs. It can be used with any of the 8080/Z-80 microcomputers running with at least 16K of RAM. Versions of CP/M for almost all 8080/Z-80 systems are available from Lifeboat Associates. The prices run between $150 and $400 for a complete package on disk.

An organization called the CP/M Users Group maintains a huge library of public domain (that means free) software. Lifeboat Associates will provide copies of the Users Group Programs for a nominal disk and copying fee. Local chapters of the CP/M Users Group can be found in many cities. A newletter, LIFELINES, is available for a yearly subscription fee. The newsletter covers the activities of local groups and product information. The address for subscriptions can be found in the appendix.

One note of caution: CP/M is a complex system that often requires considerable customizing to run exactly right. The documentation has been criticized by many. If you do not have at least some familiarity with assembler language programming, you might need a lot of help. Before you make a big financial investment, you should seek out a local users group or a computer store with some experience in the CP/M and the hardware you will be using. If you are on your own, you should either be experienced, smart, lucky, or patient. An alternative is to purchase one of the well-integrated, well-documented operating systems such as the one from North Star. The programs and languages are not as universal, but the system is easy to get on-line. Take your time and research your needs: if you then decide CP/M is for you, good luck!

CP/M allows us to use a whole world of programs on different 8080/Z-80 machines with no modification. The users group can provide disks in many different formats, but that does not help individuals who may want to exchange their own programs between computers. Disks are not completely portable between machines, so how can we get the programs inside our microcomputers without the tedious work of typing them in from the keyboard? If you are this far in the book, you know that a data communications capability feature is the obvious answer. Before we can communicate, we have to add the right pieces to our S-100/CP/M puzzle: a modem and software.

MODEMS

The most common way to attach a modem to an S-100 bus micro-computer system is through a serial port. Most systems have the serial port either built in to the computer chassis or as a part of an S-100 I/O card. If the S-100 bus microcomputer is made up of mixed-and-matched circuit boards from various manufacturers, you are absolutely on your own in developing the proper software to drive the serial port. Integrated systems, such as the North Star Horizon, are usually easier to get on the air, but customized combinations are the pride of many microcomputer users.

Once a serial board is properly interfaced, any of the RS-232-C modems on the market can deliver the data to and from the telephone line. A hybrid device such as the Racal-Vadic Modem-phone provides a good modem in a very functional package. Similarly, the Novation Auto CAT can automatically answer incoming calls at a reasonable price. Both of these devices interface through the RS-232-C port.

But there is another kind of modem device available for the user who wants even more sophisticated operating capability. RS-232-C serial connection works well for many applications, but it is a costly and inefficient way to address complex equipment. It is much more efficient to plug the modem device directly into the software bus to allow it to exchange data with the CPU in parallel form. One device designed to plug directly into the S-100 bus is the MM-103 modem from Potomac Micro-Magic.

Figure 7-2.   The Potomac Micro-Magic modem board is a very high quality device. The connector on the bottom of the card plugs into the standard S-100 bus (50 pins on each side of the card).

THE MM-103

The MM-103 is a single S-100 circuit board which connects to the
telephone line through a telephone line coupler supplied with
the unit. It will integrate with any S-100 operating system--disk,
tape, CP/M or not. If it is driven by the proper software, it
can "pick up" the telephone line, listen for a dial tone, dial
a series of numbers, listen for or transmit a carrier tone,
determine the baud rate of the system at the other end and
adjust to it, transmit data with high reliability, and hang up
the line. The baud rate, bits per word, parity mode, and number
of stop bits are all software selectable. The PMMI modem is a
versatile piece of communications equipment.
     The UART in the PMMI modem does the parallel-to-serial and
serial-to-parallel data conversion needed to interface the S-100
bus data signals to the modem chip on the circuit board. This
UART sets all the transmission parameters (baud rate, parity, and
so on) and controls the flow of characters to the modem chip by
exchanging status signals with the computer bus. The modem chip
actually generates and receives the audio tones and translates
them to and from the direct current pulses of the UART.
     A high quality set of filters is located between the modem
chip and the telephone line coupler. It filters the outgoing
tones to remove all undesired harmonics. These harmonics can
cause distortion of the signal as they pass through the amplifica-
tion and retransmission circuits of the telephone system. The
filter system also removes noise from the received signal that was
inserted on the trip over the telephone lines, and further reduces
any harmonics spilling in from the locally transmitted signal.
A modem operates like someone trying to listen and shout at the
same time--the better he can filter out the sound of his own
voice, the better he can hear. The filter circuit includes a
limiter, which clips off the tops of any noise pulses so the only
important variable in the received signal is the change in the
frequency of the received tone. This same kind of limiter
accounts for the low noise in commercial FM radio broadcasts.
There is also some logic in the filter set to switch between the
originate and answer modes.
     The telephone line coupler is an FCC-registered device that
limits hazardous voltages and unwanted tones that may enter the
telephone lines. It also protects the modem and computer system
from hazardous voltages induced in the telephone lines by electrical storms or power line accidents. The line coupler has a
relay that does the actual dial pulsing of the telephone when
dialing out. Pulse dialing will work on any telephone system in
the United States, even if push-button dialing is used.
     The dial tone detector is an unusual feature. Most other bus-
connected modem systems use a simple timer to determine when they
should start dialing. They do not listen for a dial tone; they
just assume it is there a few seconds after the line is taken off
the hook. This assumption can create problems, particularly when
dialing out through a commercial switchboard system at a school
or business where the time needed to get an outside line can be
an unknown factor. The MM-103 can be programmed to pick up the
line, listen for a dial tone, dial a digit or two, listen for
ANOTHER dial tone, and dial the complete number.

Although it is a Bell 103 standard modem, the MM-103 will operate at higher baud rates than the 300 baud usually considered to be the top end for this standard. If it is operating in the answer mode, it can recognize speeds up to 600 baud and accommodate them. In the originate mode, many large mainframe systems are able to operate faster than 300 baud, using the 103 standard. Of course, a PMMI-equipped microcomputer can be addressed at a higher speed too. There are two factors that have worked together to make 300 baud the fastest speed normally used with the 103 standard: telephone line quality and receiver reaction time. A 600 baud signal is using bits only 1,667 milliseconds long. Even a brief noise pulse on the telephone line can destroy information. The receiver of the modem must react quickly to catch each bit. The MM-103 cannot fix a noisy line, but it can filter some noise out, and the receiver can react quickly enough for 600 baud transmission.

Additionally, the MM-103 has an auxiliary interface, accessible through a connector on the top edge of the board: it provides various data and logic outputs for controlling external printers, recorders, and other equipment.

The PMMI manual contains over fifty pages of schematics, diagrams, and programs. Programs to interface the MM-103 with typical systems are included in the manual. Specific programs for some systems are available from the company on disk.

The MM-103 is a highly sophisticated device which can give a microcomputer a flexible capability. It sells for about $375. Hayes Microcomputer Products makes a version of their micromodem (described in Chapter 5) for the S-100 bus.

Figure 7-3. An S-100 bus version of the Hayes Micromodem is also available. This device is discussed in depth in the chapter dealing with the Apple II microcomputer. The S-100 version has essentially the same operating features as the unit designed for the Apple.

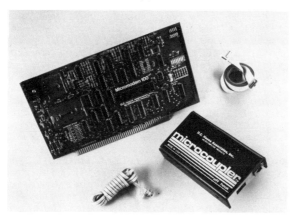

THE SOFTWARE

As good as the Potomac Micro-Magic MM-103 modem is, it--or any other modem device--cannot do much without software. There are several good programs available to run under CP/M which provide a fine communications capability. Best of all, some of them are nearly free.

The world of CP/M software is confusing. You can pay a lot of money for some commercially marketed software or very little money for a public domain program that might be just as good. Obviously, some detailed research is needed to insure that either kind of program actually meets your needs. The inexpensive program that does not do all that you want is no bargain.

BSTMS
BSTMS is an example of an expensive program. It costs about $200 on disk from Lifeboat Associates. But this program has some very specific line protocols in it to allow communications with large sophisticated host computers such as IBM, Univac, and Honeywell. It will transmit data in a format commonly used in service bureau operations, and it will transmit and receive binary files in ASCII form. BSTMS is a commercial applications program; if you need its specific capabilities, it is well worth the money.

CROSSTALK
CROSSTALK is an intelligent communications program for CP/M and North Star disk operating systems marketed by the Microstuf Company. It costs about $100 and provides a very sophisticated set of capabilities.

CROSSTALK uses specially named configuration files to store the important data about each system with which you communicate. The telephone number, baud rate, parity and stop bits, and transmission mode (half- or full-duplex) are all stored in files dedicated to each system. When you load a file, it customizes the program to the system with which you want to communicate.

The program contains a debugging mode which will display on the screen the hexidecimal value of each character being received in the modem port. This is very handy when you are trying to figure out exactly what the system at the other end is sending you in the way of control, end-of-line, or possibly special graphics characters. This is a great aid in customizing the communications system for the most efficient transmission.

CROSSTALK has an easy-to-use protocol file transfer system which can send files directly from a disk file on one system to a disk file on another CROSSTALK-equipped system. This transmission does not pass through a buffer, so it is not limited by the size of the memory available on either system. The program includes elaborate error detection, automatic retransmission, and timeout recovery.

In addition to the protocol file transfer, CROSSTALK will transmit files to almost any other electronic mail or data system using a program which compares the echoed character to the transmitted one. The program will input data into systems such as ABBS, which requires line-by-line prompted input, but it does so using a time delay instead of an actual prompt-response action. Other features include an ability to transmit files from any word processing system, a graph which shows the amount of buffer space filled with text, and a complete menu-driven command table. CROSSTALK is a capable terminal program for North Star and CP/M users. It comes in versions compatible with the Hayes and PMMI integrated modems and serial ports.

Public Domain Communications Software

The CP/M Users Group has several pieces of public domain communications software, available through local chapters or the national headquarters which shares a mailing address with Lifeboat Associates. Some fees are involved, which cover membership, service, or disks.

MODEM is certainly the most widely used CP/M communications program. It was written by Ward Christensen who, as we will discuss later, is one of the founders of the Computer Bulletin Board System. MODEM is a straightforward program allowing conversational-type terminal operation. It also has a "block mode" transmission feature which will accurately transfer files with another system running under MODEM. Checks and acknowledgements are sent from both ends and the system will try to send a block of data many times over before it gives up.

DIAL is, as you might guess, a program to dial the telephone number of a system selected from a file directory. It also contains the information needed to sign on the system. DIAL requires that the microcomputer system be equipped with an integrated modem device like those from PMMI or Hayes. It also has a conversational mode of operation.

PLINK is both a conversational and file transfer program, but it simply dumps the file out the serial port. It does not do any checking with the distant end system to verify correct receipt. This program is often known as a "despooler" because it just runs the data out like tape or string off a spool. This is a handy mode of operation and very adequate for many uses, such as electronic mail. It can be troublesome with some systems which insist on digesting data by the character or line and then calling, or prompting, for the next input.

MODEM, DIAL, and PLINK are all available from the CP/M Users Group for a nominal fee.

S-100: AN ACCEPTED STANDARD

The S-100 bus structure is far from perfect. But it has grown to be an accepted standard and its wide use is the best test of its value. Many good operating systems are available for S-100 systems. Some offer more flexibility and "off the shelf" software than others. CP/M is the most widely accepted standard operating system, but others--such as the North Star Disk Operating System-- have great popularity and are very powerful. Any S-100 bus microcomputer system can be given a sophisticated and practical communications capability. It is simply a matter of combining the right operating system, modem, and software.

Many computer manufacturers have put together integrated systems using single circuit board construction. They will be the subject of the next chapter.

chapter eight

ATARI, Heath, and Commodore Systems

The ATARI, Heath, and Commodore microcomputer systems all have the ability to serve as data communications terminals, but they have fewer options than the systems described in previous chapters. This chapter will introduce briefly each piece of equipment and describe data communications hardware and software to go with it.

ATARI

ATARI Personal Computer Systems markets two microcomputers and a complete line of peripherals and software. The ATARI 400 and the ATARI 800 use a 6502 microprocessor as the CPU. The 400 is a more economical version of the basic system with a flatfaced keyboard and limited internal memory. The 800 is a deluxe microcomputer with a full keyboard and memory expansion capability.

Both systems have standard features which might be considered extras by other manufacturers. These include upper- and lower-case characters, full screen editing with cursor control, and graphics available from the keys. They provide sixteen colors of video with eight intensities. They also contain four independent sound synthesizers for audio tones. The computers can serve as data communications terminals, but they need added hardware and software.

ATARI uses a special data bus structure to interact with peripherals such a cassette recorder and a printer. These devices connect together using an integrated cable arrangement. Connection to more standard RS-232-C devices is made through the ATARI 850 Interface Module. The 850 provides four RS-232-C ports and one eight-bit parallel output port. The 850 provides excellent expansion capability, but it is an extra cost option.

The standard ATARI configuration for communications requires the use of the 850 Interface Module and the 830 modem. The 850 Interface Module comes complete with its own power supply and connection cables. The RS-232-C ports do not use the standard DB-25 connectors. The connectors they use are less expensive and they save space, but they make it necessary to build special

Figure 8-1.   The ATARI 800 and 400 microcomputers require the use of the 850 Interface Module to provide the RS-232-C serial
port.   The ATARI 830 modem is a standard
Novation CAT wearing the ATARI label.

Figure 8-2.   The 850 Interface Module provides
four RS-232-C ports, but they do not come out
on standard DB-25 connectors.   The special cable
(right) provided with the 830 modem connects the
Interface Module to the DB-25 on the modem (left).

adapter cables if peripheral equipment is going to be switched
between the ATARI and DB-25 equipped systems. The 850 manual
provides clear information on the pin connections and such a cable
would be easy to make. ATARI has a cable which mates to a DB-25
equipped modem and it is supplied with the ATARI 830 acoustic
modem. The 830 modem is a CAT wearing the ATARI label, and the
previous description of the CAT modem applies to it.

The communications software for the ATARI 800 and 400 systems
is provided by a program called TELELINK I. TELELINK I comes in
a ROM cartridge which inserts into either computer. The program
provides for dumb terminal operation. When the transmitted or
received data scrolls off the screen it cannot be recalled, but
one option allows the transfer of the data to a printer. The
program has a full capability to transmit control codes and to
respond to control codes sent by information utilities and message
systems. These control codes are used as a part of the printer
dump routine.

TELELINK I establishes a 1.5K buffer in RAM for received data.
(The echoes of your transmissions are received data too, so actually both sides of the exchange are saved in full-duplex operation.) When the buffer is full, a special control code (XOFF or
Control S) is sent out to the system at the other end of the
telephone line. The code tells the system to stop transmitting
characters. This action insures that no data is lost during
the next step, which is a dump of data to the printer. The program moves the data from the buffer to the printer, clears the
buffer, and sends another control code (XON or Control Q) to the
distant system to tell it to resume sending. This action takes
some time, and time--on many systems--is money paid for system
use, long distance telephone bills, or both.

A manual mode of operation is available. In manual operation,
the operator can keep the buffer closed (and the printer off)
until some interesting data is about to be transmitted. Then the
buffer can be opened and the data stored and dumped to the printer.
This mode is useful since it greatly reduces the time needed and
the action of the printer. But the operator has to know that the
information to be saved is coming before it appears on the screen,
so the buffer can be opened.

The ATARI computers (and any other computers using a video
modulator to connect to a television set instead of a monitor)
can only display about thirty-two characters in one line of data
on the screen. TELELINK I wraps around words in lines longer
than thirty-two characters, so the words are not broken. An
adapter cable is available which will allow an ATARI computer to
send video to a color or black and white video monitor.

The TELELINK I program is a first step in data communications
software. ATARI has a more sophisticated program under development and more software will be coming from independent companies.
The ATARI software library now includes a very powerful word processing package, and a similar terminal program will round out the
appeal of the ATARI 400 and 800 for hobby, educational, and business users.

The Microperipheral Corporation markets a version of the Microconnection modem device for the ATARI systems. The Microconnection allows data communications operation without the use of the 850 Interface Module. It also provides a separate RS-232-C port, which allows the direct connection of a printer which can simultaneously copy along with the received data stream without the need for the store-and-dump routine. Software supplied on a cassette provides a communications program addressed to the Microconnection's data location. The TELELINK I software will not properly address the Microconnection. This device provides an alternative method for turning an ATARI microcomputer into a data communications terminal.

HEATH H-89 (Z-89)

The Heath Company has a flexible computer system available in kit form known as the H-89.

Figure 8-3. The H-89 "All in One" microcomputer combines a terminal, powerful
microcomputer, and disk drive in one
cabinet. It operates as a full function
terminal with no additional software, but
a good terminal program integrates the
system into a complete smart terminal
system. (Photo courtesy of Heath Co.)

The same system is available assembled from Zenith as the Z-89. The H-89 computer system is actually a hybrid device in one well-integrated package.

The system has two separate parts which share only a common cabinet and power supply. The first part is a high quality data communications terminal with many powerful features, including full screen cursor control, editing, eighty-character lines, and special function keys. This is essentially a repackaging of the successful Heath H-19 terminal. The terminal contains its own

Z-80 microprocessor and operating system. It also has an RS-232-C
port and, indeed, communicates with its siamese twin computer over
an RS-232-C link.

   The computer portion of the H-89 uses a Z-80 as a CPU. It
has a built-in disk drive and the ability to carry 64K of internal
memory. Additional disk drives and printers are available to add
to the system. An optional RS-232-C serial I/O board is needed to
interface with a modem.

   H-89 users can have an excellent data communications system
in either of two ways. The terminal portion of the H-89 can
interface with a modem directly. It operates as a smart terminal
with a full eighty-key keyboard, including all control codes and
even a numeric pad. Of course, it will not save data in files and
it cannot read local files in this configuration. The terminal
can provide a professional level of operation for many uses by
itself.

   For more sophisticated operation, the terminal can be
connected to the computer, and the combined H-89 package can
utilize one of the best intelligent terminal programs available.
REACH is a very sophisticated program written by Walter Bilofsky
and distributed by Software Toolworks.

   The minimum hardware required to run REACH is an H-89, 16K of
memory, an H88-3 serial interface, and a modem. REACH supports up
to 48K of memory and most printers. The program operates under
the Heath Disk Operating System.

   REACH fits every definition of a smart terminal program.
It will save data in specially named files, transmit data from
files, respond to prompts for transmission by line or by character, send automatic sign-on or other commonly used character
strings, and provide many convenient operating features. Program
operation is made extremely simply by the use of the special function keys on the H-89 keyboard. Simply pressing one of the function keys (F1-F5) sets an operating mode for the program.

   As an example, to transfer data from a disk file to a remote
computer, the operator simply presses the F3 special function key.
The program asks for the file name. When the operator responds,
the file is sent using one of four selectable transmission formats
or rates.

   Saving received data is equally simple. The operator presses
the F2 key, names a file, and the received data is saved into that
file when the buffer is full. If a printer is connected to the
H-89, REACH can print the received characters at the same time
they are displayed on the screen. REACH is set to operate with
the most common Heath printers.

COMMODORE PET/CBM

Commodore Business Machines (CBM) introduced one of the first
practical microcomputers in the Commodore PET. The PET has been
followed by a complete line of computers, including the most
powerful CBM machines. There are many models of PETs, and there
are even differences within models, caused by different operating
systems contained in ROM. The information provided in this
chapter will apply generally to all PET/CBM machines.

PET/CBM owners face a double handicap when they try to use their systems as communications devices. First, the interface to the outside world for PET systems is not the RS-232-C standard. Second, it is not "real" ASCII.

Commodore chose to use IEEE standard 488-1975 as an electrical standard for the connection of peripherals. The IEEE 488 port is not a serial port. Data is transmitted in an eight-bit parallel format. IEEE 488 is most commonly used to interconnect programmable test instruments in industry and in laboratories. It is also known as the Hewlett-Packard Instrument Bus (HP-IB).

Modems are available commercially to interface with this standard, but they are instrument grade devices which are usually much more expensive than the more common RS-232-C modems. The most economical way to connect to a more common modem is to convert the IEEE 488 parallel signals into RS-232-C serial signals. We will look at a device which does this and also at at a complete integrated IEEE 488/Bell 103 modem device.

But, first, we must deal with the second nonstandard aspect of PET operation. Most PET computers do not have extensive keyboards. Some have so-called graphic keyboards which have graphic figures directly available from the keys. These graphic characters are available through the use of the shift key. The PET character coding is the same as ASCII for all "unshifted" characters (capital letters and numbers), but shifted characters (graphics and lower case) do not correspond to the ASCII standard coding. The communications software or hardware must do a great deal of conversion if these systems can be used effectively with full ASCII data communications networks. Some CBM computers have "business" keyboards which are less of a problem, but they still do not produce or recognize all characters or any control codes.

However, TNW Corporation has several different hardware and software packages giving the PET/CBM full flexibility to communicate as a smart terminal using an available RS-232-C modem or an integrated IEEE 488/Bell 103 modem package.

The TNW-1000 serial interface is a single circuit board which is physically mounted on the back of the PET/CBM microcomputer. It contains its own power supply and it is very simple to install. The TNW-1000 translates between the IEEE 488 parallel data port and the IEEE RS-232-C serial data stream. The unit can operate over a variety of speeds and with the usual selection of RS-232-C transmission options (parity, and so on). It is important to note that this serial interface also translates the PET/CBM character set to standard ASCII. This device sells for about $130 and gives the PET/CBM computers a good communications capability. The TNW-1000 would, of course, be used to interface with some sort of RS-232-C/Bell 103 modem for connection to the telephone system.

TNW also makes a complete IEEE 488/Bell 103 modem with direct connect capabilities to allow auto-answer and auto-dial operation. The TNW 488/103 is a sophisticated device that plugs directly into the PET/CBM microcomputer. Software for terminal operations is included on a cassette with the TNW 488/103. The PTERM software package will operate in an 8K PET. The complete integrated modem sells for about $400. PTERM is available separately for about $20.

If you are serious about communicating with a PET/CBM machine, you should at least invest in the Documentation Package for the TNW 488/103 modem. This is a typewritten fifty-page pamphlet, full of definitions and practical descriptions of how the Commodore microcomputers communicate. It is certainly the single best available source of information on PET/CBM data communications interfaces.

TNW makes other data communications devices similar to the ones described above. These include a self-contained 488/232 adapter, a Bell standard 212 modem, and a full line of IEEE 488, PET/CBM, and RS-232-C cables. An upgraded version of the PTERM software to interface with disk systems is also available.

If you need an eight-bit parallel port (used by many printers) along with an RS-232-C port, Connecticut microComputer manufactures a device called SADI which can provide both the standard serial and standard parallel interfaces. SADI is a simultaneous data interface which performs the same sort of ASCII translation done by the TNW devices. SADI sells for about $300. SADI needs a standard RS-232-C modem to connect to the telephone lines.

PET and Commodore Business Machines microcomputers can make effective data communications terminals. They do not use the interface standards most commonly used by other systems, but equipment is available to translate to the common standard.

chapter nine

Microcomputer-Based Message Systems

The early chapters of this book introduced the concept of the Time Tyranny of Telecommunications. Defeating this time tyranny requires some form of store-and-forward message system which will hold data messages until the addressee desires delivery. While some different kinds of store-and-forward systems--including telephone answering machines--are now popular, they do not provide all the advantages of a data communications electronic message system. A message system should make entry and retrieval of messages as simple as possible, and be able to transfer something more than just messages.

A store-and-forward message system has many practical applications in commerce, industry, education, and training. Traveling sales personnel can dial into such a system at the end of a day's work and pick up calls, leave orders, and skim the latest market and sales information. This can be done without detaining or employing people at the main office to answer telephones and take messages. Special programs can be available on the system to help figure orders, costs, or commissions. An excellent microcomputer system that can do this costs less than $5000.

Industry can use a store-and-forward message system for any group of individuals in different locations working on similar projects. Development teams and project teams can trade information, receive assignments, and keep track of progress using a dial-up message system. Software teams can exchange complete listings or actually demonstrate running programs on the same system.

A message system is an outstanding educational tool for every level from high school through graduate school. High school students can achieve a degree of computer literacy through interaction with a computer system shared by a class. College and graduate students can exchange class notes, consult with faculty advisors, and run special programs. Evening and correspondence students can benefit from having a class forum available whenever they need it.

All these applications--and many more--can be met with a microcomputer-based electronic message system. Several hundred electronic message systems are in operation throughout the world, mainly in the United States and Canada, but systems have been reported operational in France, Korea, England, Holland, Australia, and Japan. These systems vary in complexity and degree of service.

Some run on sophisticated minicomputers with many megabytes of disk storage space available. Others use simple single board microcomputers and programs which store messages only in the available RAM. Some are able to exchange programs with users, provide protected mail service, and even provide elegant subsystems for the use of special interest groups. Some systems consider themselves national in scope; others serve a few friends living in a local neighborhood. Microcomputer-based message systems are used by large corporations, small shops, private special interest groups, and clubs of all types.

THE SYSTEM OPERATOR (SYSOP)

Someone has got to take care of the darn thing! Although electronic message systems run unattended, they still require regular "care and feeding." After a system is operational, the system operator (SYSOP) will probably spend a minimum of thirty minutes a day killing old messages, responding to new ones, and compacting message files.

Most SYSOPs supply everything free--the computer, the power, the telephone line, and the disk--because they enjoy serving, or because they like being a part of all the action.

The average message system in a metropolitan area has about thirty to forty callers a day. Some have many more. Many callers are young people using terminals at local schools. Others have varying levels of expertise in microcomputer systems. Thanks to the efforts of the SYSOPs, the callers can share knowledge and ideas that transcend the usual cultural and social barriers.

This chapter will describe the history, use, and setup of the most common types of microcomputer-based message systems. First, let us see where it all started.

CBBS #1

Two men living in the Chicago area--Ward Christensen and Randy Suess--were early users of microcomputer systems. In 1977, they began communicating between their systems to software and messages. In early 1978, Christensen wrote the software for a kind of electronic bulletin board which would replace the actual cork bulletin board used at a local computer club. This system was to work exactly like a cork and thumbtack bulletin board. People entering the computer through the telephone lines could browse through the notes and see what equipment might be for sale, who needed help, and so on. They could leave notes in reply and destroy their own notes after they had lost their usefulness. Seuss put together the microcomputer hardware, and the first Computer Bulletin Board System (CBBS) was born.

At the time, electronic mail systems were available on several large mainframe computer systems, but Christensen and Seuss, in effect, reinvented the wheel for microcomputer-based systems. By the middle of 1978, four CBBS computers were in operation. The number has grown to over a dozen, but there is a frequent changeover of systems as individuals gain or lose time, equipment, or interest.

ABBS

In 1979, the Apple computer grew rapidly in popularity. Two men in California shared an idea for setting up an electronic message system based on Apple hardware. Craig Vaughan seems to have developed the original approach. Bill Blue did the operational and human engineering of the software, and the product was marketed through a California firm and through computer stores. This began the Apple Bulletin Board System (ABBS). Because of the availability of the software and the popularity of the hardware, there are usually more ABBS computers in operation at any given time than any other kind of system. These are often hobby systems run by individuals, and their operation may not be as consistent or as permanent as other systems.

FORUM 80

With the popularity of the TRS-80 computer (particularly the version now known as the TRS-80 Model I), it was inevitable that good message system software would appear for that hardware. Bill Abney in Kansas City, Missouri, wrote a program he calls Forum 80 for this system. Abney has kept close control over the Forum 80 operation, and the various operators around the country cooperate closely in updating software and maintaining standard methods of operation for the users.

OTHER SYSTEMS

Many other kinds of microcomputer-based message systems now exist. The availability of less expensive auto-answer modems has made interface to the telephone system reasonably easy. The protocols have been initially established and the method of operation refined. Now that the ground has been broken, almost any decent programmer can develop a message program in BASIC that allowed will perform elementary message filing and display functions. However, the first developers deserve a great deal of credit for taking the lead and providing the software and organization that allowed hundreds of thousands of terminal users to enter the world of personal data communications for the first time.

USING A MESSAGE SYSTEM

Successful initial use of an electronic message system depends 10% on technical skill, 20% on terminal equipment, and 70% on psychology. Many technically skilled persons freeze when a computer asks them their name. Some of the best computer communications users are liberal arts majors in college and nontechnical students in high schools. Later, experience replaces psychology, but technical skill is never a large factor in the use of electronic message systems.

Many persons, it seems, are either afraid of causing damage to the distant end computer system by giving it incorrect commands or they are afraid of looking foolish to the machine. Neither fear is justified. The operating programs for all successful message systems have been refined to the point where they cannot be broken, even by deliberate malicious action. In fact, they are loaded with help commands and useful prompts to direct inexperienced users. Inexperienced users should not be embarrassed. It is true that SYSOPs often watch users operate the systems (this is referred to as the "Big Brother position"), but this is usually with an eye toward monitoring the hardware operation and improving the functioning of the software. If you ever do manage to show the SYSOP a problem, you will probably be met with gratitude. So, when trying a system for the first time, or when introducing others to the world of data communications, remember: you cannot break the computer, nor will it laugh at you! It is indestructible and it has nearly infinite patience.

Sign-on

Now that we have developed the proper psychological attitude, let us see how we go about entering and using an electronic message system. The systems are not standardized, so this description will be given in general terms with some explanation of the exceptions.
The first step is to properly set up your terminal or your microcomputer serving as a terminal. You should be operating as a terminal in the full-duplex (echo-plex) mode with upper-case-only characters selected. Some message systems and information utilities will not accept commands in lower-case characters. Your system should be set to 300 baud, seven-bit words, even parity, and one stop bit. Your modem should be on the originate mode with full-duplex selected. Now you are ready to dial the telephone.
Some terminal hardware/software combinations will dial the telephone for you on command, but let us assume we are using a simple system with an acoustic coupler. As the number gets ready to ring, you should listen to the quality of the telephone line. If there is a great deal of noise, you might consider hanging up and redialing in an attempt to get a better circuit. Remember, your modem will have to detect changes in tones that happen in about three milliseconds. If the telephone line has a lot of noise, those changes could be masked. If the number is not busy, the system should answer within three rings. Four or five rings without an answer indicates the system is not operational.
The system should answer with a high pitch tone. This is the constant tone coming from a modem in the answer mode. Most systems will only wait about eight to ten seconds without receiving a tone in return before it assumes your call is a wrong number and disconnects. Your modem will take a second or so to recognize the tone and reply, so do not delay too long in placing the telephone instrument in the modem cups or cutting the direct connect modem into the circuit. If you are using an acoustic modem, make sure you put the handset in the right way! An arrow will often point toward the end of the modem at which the handset's cord should be placed. Also, an acoustic modem must be used in a reasonably quiet area. A radio or a noisy printer can inject unacceptable noise into the handset and modem. Once connected, your modem should respond to the tone and light up READY or CARRIER, or give some other indication that it is working.

The first words you see on your screen will probably be some variation of HIT CR. The message system needs to see a few of your carriage returns (the ENTER or RETURN key) so it can tell what speed you are using. Some systems still support 110 baud and several support speeds up to 600 baud: the system needs to know how fast you are going so it can set itself to match your speed. The next question will be:

TERMINAL NEED NULLS?

This question is important if you are using a printing terminal. Many printing terminals need nulls or blanks after a carriage return and line feed to allow the print head enough time to return to the left side of the page. If this is not a problem, you can probably ignore this question and it will go away. If it does not go away, simply hit RETURN. If you are using a slow printing terminal, follow the directions (type YES or enter control N) and the system will enter nulls. If you are asked how many nulls, try answering 5. You may have to experiment with this number until you get good print head return with little idle time.

Forum 80 systems may also ask if you want line feeds. Line feeds move the paper up in a printer (or the cursor down on a screen) and are not always associated with carriage returns. This is a function of your software. Some software always generates an internal line feed when it does a carriage return. Some software does not. You are safe answering YES to this question. The most that can happen is that you get double spaced lines which are easy to read but scroll off the screen fast. If you answer NO, you may find all your data printing over itself on one line.

You will be asked to enter your first name, last name, and the location from which you are calling. If you have not been on the system before, your name will be added to a log file. You may be asked for specific information about your terminal equipment. The system may ask if you can use lower-case characters, how many characters you can display in a line of data, and other information. This will be kept on file with your name and the next time you sign on, the system will know you and treat you accordingly.

Certain systems may interrogate your terminal software to determine if you are using a program with special features the system recognizes. An example of this is the Forum 80 message system and ST80-III terminal software. Each copy of ST80-III can automatically tell the Forum 80 what its unique software serial number is for purposes of sure recognition during sign-on.

The next thing you see on your screen will certainly be the welcome message and system announcements. The announcements may be any information of interest to the operator and users. They will also probably include information on the control characters or special commands that the system accepts. Some systems have expanded files of historical and system configuration data. You may be interested in browsing through later, but for now let us move on to the place where the business is done: the command line.

Commands and Control Codes

Most of the electronic message systems (CBBS, ABBS, and so on) use similar top level commands. These are the first command choices you will make. Since there is no formal standard, we will examine a typical command line and see what the more common commands do. A typical command line might be

FUNCTION: B,C,D,E,G,H,K,O,Q,R,S,X,?

The command line wants you to enter a letter to tell the system what to do. If you are confused or you do not remember the commands you want, you can always enter H (Help) and the system will provide you with help in understanding the commands for the level of the program you are on. Here is what some of the other commands mean:

B Entering this letter will display the bulletins which you might have seen at sign-on. A longer historical list of bulletins might also be displayed.

C This is the case switch. It changes operation of the system from upper case to combined upper and lower case, or vice versa. This is a toggle operation. Each time a C is entered, the system is toggled from one mode of operation to the other.

D The D command toggles between full- and half-duplex (echo/no echo). Echo is the normal or "default" operating mode.

E This tells the system you want to enter a message. You will be asked to specify to whom the message is going and what the sub- ject is. You should do this in upper case and in a standard form (for example, "TRS-80," not "trs 80") so others who use a system scan for messages of interest will not miss yours.

G This says goodbye. This initiates the sign-off to end the session. Special Note: A "T" for "Terminate" is used by Forum 80 systems to end the session. Sending a Forum 80 a "G" puts you into the graphics mode of operation which can greatly confuse non-TRS-80 terminals. A sign-off command should be sent to all systems. You should never simply hang up because the system may wait for input from you for several minutes before recycling. During that time it would not be available for other users.

K The K command is sent to tell the system you want to "kill" a message. Often messages are "locked" with a password, so you may not be able to kill messages you did not originate or for which you do not know the password.

O This stands for "other" systems. This normally provides a de- tailed listing of other message systems around the country. The accuracy of the list varies with the kind of system you are on and the concern of the SYSOP who must make all the entries and correc- tions. Generally, a Forum 80 system will have an accurate listing of all other Forum 80s. The only other generalization that can be made is that a large percentage of the telephone numbers listed on any system are no longer active--despite the most dedicated ef- forts of the SYSOP.

Q The system will present a "quick" summary of messages, including only information such as who the message is from and to whom it is sent.

R This command allows you to "retrieve" a message from the file for reading. You will be asked for the message number, so you probably will have to execute the Q or S instructions first. Various suboptions under the R command may allow you to retrieve multiple messages sequentially or messages you flagged for retrieval on a previous scan.

S This commands a more detailed "summary" which includes the subject, the date entered, and possibly the length of the message. Often, scanning can be done selectively. You might wish to scan for all messages with your name in the TO line, or all messages with Apple in the SUBJECT line. Directions for performing a selective scan are usually contained in the HELP file. Some systems have so many messages on file that you might also be asked what block of messages (by message number) you wish to scan.

X An X command indicates an "expert" mode of operation. The system skips long prompts and "hand-holding." It assumes you are an experienced system user.

If the system you check into is anything but a Forum 80, one of the notices that may appear in the sign-on and introduction is probably

CONTROL CHARACTERS ACCEPTED BY THIS SYSTEM

This is accompanied by a quick list of control characters and their functions. Control characters are important to the smooth operation of many systems because they provide an executive level of control. The ability to transmit control characters is advantageous for this reason. Forum 80s do not recognize control characters because the early TRS-80 terminal software did not produce them. The most commonly used control (CTL) characters are:

CTL C (Cancel) This command may either cancel the current line being sent or the entire message currently being printed.

CTL K (Kill) This kills the current function (Scanning, Reading, and so on). Operation may return to the command line or to the next logical function if you are down in a subsystem.

CTL N (Nulls) Send nulls after a carriage return.

CTL S (Stop) This control is also called XOFF. It stops the distant system from sending you any more characters. This is handy if you want to study something on the screen, make notes, answer the doorbell, and so on. On some systems, another CTL S is needed to restart transmission. Other systems will resume when any new character is received from you (hit any key). The standard response is CTL Q.

CTL Q   This control, also called XON, is used by many systems (including Source and Compuserve) to signal a restart of transmission after a CTL S.

Several other control codes may be used for purposes such as flagging (CTL F) messages for later retrieval and canceling all functions (CTL X) which causes a return to the command line.
The commands and control codes listed above are the ones in most general use. Many systems have additional commands available. Also, certain commands may have different meanings at different program function levels. The S command, for instance, means "scan" at the top (initial sign-on) level of the operating program. But during the formulation and entry of a message (a lower command level) the S may cause the message to be "saved" to disk. Similarly, an E command may become "edit" instead of "enter." This reuse of the same letter command is usually not confusing because detailed prompts are provided to the user. The "?" or "Help" request will usually bring a clear explanation of a command's meaning at that functional level.
Each type of message system has its own particular short cuts and its own operating conveniences. Some systems allow you to "stack" your commands or responses all on one line to speed entry. This presumes the user knows what questions the program will ask. The questions the program asks can be answered before they are displayed if the answers are separated by a semicolon. As an example, experience may have shown that a CBBS asks the following questions in the following order:

IS THIS YOUR FIRST TIME ON THE SYSTEM?,
FIRST NAME?
LAST NAME?
All three questions can be answered on one line. A typical stacked entry line might be
(computer sends) FIRST TIME?
(you reply) N; FRED; RALPHSON

Stacking commands can be used in other situations. You may have learned that the system you use responds to a retrieve command with the questions

MULTIPLE RETRIEVAL?,   and then
MESSSAGE NUMBER?

Your stacked input line might be

R;N;22

which tells the computer you want to retrieve the single message numbered 22. The single "N" above in both cases is shorthand for "no." Similarly, a "Y" represents "yes."
Some systems cater to their regular users. Frequent users can often arrange with the SYSOP to provide special privileges such as private message listings, auto log-on numbers, or access to the master files.
Many systems have a program upload and download feature. This turns the message system into an electronic program exchange.

Various utility and game programs are available free of charge to system users. Users are encouraged to contribute personal or non-copyrighted public domain programs for the use of others. A smart terminal program is required to save the received program for later reuse. Many message systems allow the user to run resident programs. This is more of a classic computer utility function, but it is a valuable service for persons using a standard terminal or a microcomputer-based terminal with a RAM space too small to run the desired program.

Special interest message systems are also popular. These special interest systems range in type from those dedicated to technically oriented users of the CP/M operating system to those designed for persons interested in geneaology. Other systems dedicated to avionics, various kinds of medical education, photography, amateur radio, engineering, and computer game playing have all been established.

Using the special features of microcomputer-based message systems is not difficult. A great deal of effort has been expended in rendering systems easy to use. A careful reading of the HELP commands and a little practice will lead to a very enjoyable data communications experience.

SETTING UP AN ELECTRONIC MESSAGE SYSTEM

Establishing an electronic message system can simply involve the combination of some readily available hardware and software. In order to determine what hardware and software are best for a particular application, two questions must be answered: 1) What is the purpose of the system? and 2) What hardware is available?

Determing the actual purpose of the system involves a study of what services are needed, how many users and messages may be handled, and any special features desired, such as privacy, different data alphabets, and so on. If cost is a major factor, then the use of available hardware may be a big consideration. Large message systems can use a great deal of disk space, and high capacity disk systems can be expensive. Fortunately, some less expensive combinations of hardware can be used.

Remote Operation

The simplest sort of message system is called remote operation. In this kind of system, the microcomputer is made available for remote entry and operation through the RS-232-C port. The serial port is, in effect, placed in parallel across the local keyboard by the software. Data coming in from the serial port is displayed and acted upon just as if it were entered locally. Remote operation can be extended any distance by the use of a modem and the telephone lines.

During remote operation, programs in RAM or those available on disk can be run as long as they do not 1) contain machine language subroutines which are incompatible with the remote operation program or 2) require local physical actions such as the changing of disks. In the most elementary forms, messages could be left on a system like this in the form of BASIC programs full of REM or PRINT statements. Programs could be LISTed or RUN to read the text.

The Hayes Micromodem and PMMI modem boards have the ability to interface with the telephone line, answer the ring, and provide this remote operation feature. Many other modems, including the Microconnection and others have an auto-answer function which will at least answer the telephone under software control. Apple II, S-100 bus, and TRS-80 microcomputer systems are all easily provided with a remote operation feature.

A simple program is available to allow remote operation of the TRS-80 Model I. The COMMUNICATOR from Instant Software is a cassette-based program that provides complete remote operation of a TRS-80 through the RS-232-C port. The program resides in high memory and does all the interface necessary to serve as a computer utility, including echoing received characters. It does not include the routines needed to answer and hang up the telephone line through the modem.

Two other programs are available for the TRS-80 Model I which allow message system operation with the most simple Level II 16K keyboard-only system. Both require the use of the Microconnection modem device with the Autoconnection option. SUPERHOST provides full remote operation with telephone answering and hang-up under program control. MINI-MSG is a more complete message system program which actually functions as a bulletin board. Users are greeted on sign-on and can read all messages or enter messages of their own. It runs completely in RAM and stores all messages in RAM. No disk or cassette storage is needed. RAM-only storage provides a practical limit on the size or length of the messages available, but a 16K system can serve the needs of a surprisingly large community of users if messages are kept brief. RAM-only storage also means all messages are lost if the power fails. The program would be ideal for any small business, school, or club that would like to operate its own electronic message system at minimum cost. SUPERHOST sells for about $30 and MINI-MSG for $50 from the Microperipheral Corporation. Both programs address the Microconnection ports and will not work with other modem devices.

Lance Micklus has written a practical program which includes a message bulletin board, runs in a 16K machine, and addresses the standard TRS-80 ports. ST80-X10 is essentially a machine language program that allows remote operation. It runs with a BASIC language bulletin board program called ST80-PBB. ST80-PBB even includes two computer games to give your users something to do after they have read the messages. The BASIC language message program has options for various levels of entry by users. Users may be required to provide a system password for full entry into the message storage or program area. "Guest" users may be allowed limited entry without a password. They can, for instance, be limited to leaving messages only to the SYSOP. This kind of system has good commercial applications for taking sales orders or selling information, such as stock tips. It could also be useful in training and education. The programs can run on the TRS-80 Model I and Model III tape or disk systems. A more sophisticated message system program, ST80-CC, is also available.

Sophisticated Electronic Message Systems
Trying to describe sophisticated electronic message systems in detail is somewhat like trying to describe the patterns of flames in a fireplace. You know they are warm and complex and beautiful,

but they keep changing. The people who write message system software do so mainly for the love of it. They try to keep commonality and to provide good documentation, but they are very similar to artists who must add just one more brush stroke to their work and who often wind up repainting large sections of canvas. However, those conditions notwithstanding, in this section we will look at several sophisticated message system programs, describe the hardware needed to run them, and tell where they are available.

Several of the best message system packages are not for sale as money-making products; they are available for a cost which does not reflect the work that went into them. But they are also available without the "handholding" and support expected from a software distributor selling a major program. The authors might also want some control over their use. Let us look first at the CBBS software.

The CBBS program, written by Ward Christensen, runs under the CP/M operating system. It comes on two eight-inch floppy disks which contain many thousands of lines of machine language code. The CP/M operating system must, of course, be purchased separately and be fully integrated with the hardware.

The hardware requirements to run the system are an S-100-based microcomputer system with a Z-80 or 8080 CPU, at least 24K of RAM, a disk system, and an auto-answer modem. An integrated modem such as the Hayes or PMMI is preferred. A minimum of 70K of disk space is required and much more is really advisable. Although the program is written to run under CP/M, and that operating system is certainly not restricted to S-100 bus machines, the program is designed to run on an S-100 system.

This program may require some degree of experience or patience to bring up with different hardware configurations. The price is kept low ($50) because the system developers do not have the time to help every person who might try to bring a system on-line. Common hardware configurations using the PMMI or Hayes modem devices can be brought up quickly, but bringing any special requirements or configurations on-line may require a good knowledge of CP/M and machine language code.

Forum 80
The Forum 80 system is referred to as a "network" by its creator, William Abney. The various Forums are not interconnected electrically as a true network might be, but they are connected in commonality of software and exchange of information on a regular basis. The Forum 80 software is not for sale. Forum 80 operators pay a one-time license fee for the use of the program, but control of the program remains with Abney. Specialized features such as program uploading and downloading, and submenus for special interest user groups, are available.

A typical Forum 80 requires a TRS-80 Model I, 48K of RAM, and four disk drives. An auto-answer modem is required.

A commercial version of the electronic message system software written by Abney is reported to be under development.

MESSAGE 80
A slightly less sophisticated, but more readily available, program for the TRS-80 is called MESSAGE 80. This program, written

by Richard Taylor, is designed to be very flexible. It can easily be modified for selling software on-line, or for use as a remote data base, a company message system, or a more conventional electronic message system. It requires a TRS-80 Model I or III, at least two disk drives (depending on the application), 48K of memory, RS-232-C interface, and an auto-answer modem. Versions are available for the standard RS-232-C port address, or the Microconnection with the Autoconnection option.

MESSAGE 80 sells for about $150 from the Microperipheral Corporation.

ABBS

The Apple Bulletin Board System software is certainly the most widely used electronic message system program. The software is easy to bring on-line and does not require extraordinarily large disk capacity. The hardware package for an ABBS typically consists of an Apple II Plus or Apple II with AppleSoft in ROM, a Hayes Micromodem II, and at least one disk drive. An additional disk drive is needed if any optional program features are used. The software can also support large capacity hard disk storage systems.

The ABBS software is supplied on two separate disks which contain various system configuration routines. The user is, in effect, taken by the hand and led through a series of steps which customize the software to the available hardware and desired operating parameters.

There are many optional features available for the ABBS system software. Program exchange is one of the most popular features. Users of the message system can download programs to their own terminal and save them for later use. They can also upload programs into the message system so that others can borrow them.

Another valuable option includes special user "conferences." These conferences are actually message subsystems for special interest groups. They can be given any names desired and are available as an option from the command line.

Craig Vaughan markets the ABBS software and other related communications programs through Software Sorcery. The initial software package sells for about $70. With options the total cost can be over $150, but this price is low considering the quality and ease of use of the software. Vaughan also has programs with greater security options for corporate users and communications programs for users of the Pascal programming language.

People's Message System

The People's Message System is a bulletin board system using software written by Bill Blue. The software is designed to run on the Apple II Plus computer equipped with the Hayes Micromodem II. It can be operated on as little as two Apple minidrives, and it is upwardly expandable to eight-inch drives or a hard disk system. The primary system can accommodate up to 116 messages, but the system will automatically purge old messages as new ones are entered. Additional messages can be stored if more disk space is available.

A separate file for news or system bulletins is available, as is a features section for providing on-line articles, advertising, club news, or any other features of interest. Blue has even included an "obscene filter" in this system. This filter consists of a file on one disk containing all the words or phrases which the operator does not wish to be displayed. Each message saved to disk is checked against this file and if any matches are found, the message will not be saved.

The People's Message System has many other features such as the ability to assign "accounts" to frequent users, and to allow users to upload and download programs. These features are in extensive service. This program comes individually configured for each installation and costs between $200 and $300, depending on options.

North Star

The Microstuf company has a bulletin board system which is written in North Star Basic. The program package, called "Bulletin Board" is actually a series of programs including the message program itself, a log-on program, menu and help programs, and a utility program to pack the disk files. The package looks like one integrated program to the user and is easy to install on a Horizon computer. Selected users may gain access to BASIC language programs in the computer and run other programs, but only under control of the Bulletin Board package.

Versions of "Bulletin Board" are available for the PMMI and Hayes integral modems. A version operating in Microsoft BASIC under CP/M is also available. The "Bulletin Board" (with its accessory remote access program) sells for about $100.

PET and CBM

Fred Hambrecht deserves credit for putting the first PET Bulletin Board System on the air. The PBBS software can run in a 16K PET or CBM with one disk. Either the TNW 2000 or the TNW 488/103 serial port devices described in Chapter 8 is required. The message system software is available for about $25 with extra cost options available.

Microcomputer-based electronic message systems of all kinds are a new phenomenon in the world of communications. They grow, change, and have impact on the world around them with amazing speed. Their uses are only as limited as the imaginations of the people who program and operate them.

One of the most humanitarian of all message system uses is as a communications medium for handicapped individuals. The next chapter deals with message systems for the deaf.

chapter ten

Communications
for the Deaf

Perhaps no group of people can benefit more from data communication systems than the deaf and the hearing-impaired. Deaf
people need a way to communicate that is not based on sound.
Unfortunately, the technologies first developed in the communications revolution--telephone and radio--depended completely on
sound. Throughout the twentieth century, deaf people have been
culturally isolated because of the importance of sound to society.

If you are deaf, how do you call your boss to say you will
be late for work? If you are deaf, how do you call the police,
obtain a driver's license, pay an electric bill, and so on? How
do you receive warning of severe weather conditions or utility
outages? Quite frankly, you do not.

The deaf have been using electrical data communications
equipment since the 1960s. Ironically, this early establishment
of a transmission method has actually worked against their partic-
ipation in data communications developments that are based on the
microprocessor.

In 1968, an agreement was negotiated between the Alexander
Graham Bell Association of the Deaf (in Washington, D.C.) and
American Telephone & Telegraph (AT&T). It was agreed that AT&T
would provide deaf persons with surplus Model 15 teleprinters.
(Teleprinters are also known generically as TTY or "teletype"
machines--"Teletype" is a trademark of the Teletype Corporation.)
AT&T and the communications carriers served as a source of these
machines through the late 1970s.

Most of the machines were used by deaf persons in a point-
to-point mode. The surplus machines were installed in homes,
schools, businesses, and even some police stations. This was
probably the first large scale use of data systems for personal
communications. Deaf persons could actually call their friends
and "chat" by long distance, or call schools or civil authorities
for help. Estimates placed the number of deaf people using data
communications devices at over 77,000 by the end of the 1970s.
(There are about 2.4 million deaf people in the United States.)

The technology used in these communications schemes predates
World War II. The teleprinter I/O port is a direct current interconnect to electromagnets which push on typebars attached to the
typehead. The coding of the DC line is done in a five-bit code
referred to as Baudot or Murray code (see Chapter 2). Timing for
the reception and transmission of the bits is done by DC motors.

The speed of transmission is typically 60 WPM OR 45.45 baud.
The modem used to send the data over the telephone line is
called a Weitbrecht modem. Only two tones are used over the transmission path--1400 Hz mark and 1800 Hz space. In the Weitbrecht
modem, tones are only transmitted for the duration of the character so that the line is available for transmission in either
direction between characters. In practice, the mark tone is held
for as long as a second before it is dropped to provide continuity
while continuous strings of characters are transmitted.

Deaf communicators have come under various pressures in the
1980s. Time and technology seem to be working against them.
Their mechanically complex teleprinters are wearing out and parts
are difficult to find. Technology has turned in another direction,
and ASCII coding at speeds of 300, 600, and 1200 baud has become
standard. Services such as information utilities, which would
meet many needs for deaf people, do not usually interface with
their machines. Many deaf persons simply cannot afford to buy a
microcomputer to rejoin the data communications revolution. Those
that can afford new equipment hesitate to leave their friends with
60 WPM Baudot-coded devices behind.

One obvious solution would be to provide microcomputers which
serve a message systems and as terminals with a Baudot code
capability, along with their ASCII capability. We have seen
several programs using translation tables which can essentially
turn an ASCII-coded character into any other ASCII-coded or non-
ASCII coded character instantly. This translation is easily done
in software. But the major problem is not coding; it is speed.
The designers of the integrated circuit devices in use today did
not provide for speeds below 110 baud. Some special hardware and
software magic must be worked to meet the lower speed standard for
the deaf.

One group has been working hard to produce this magic. The
Amateur Radio Research and Development Corporation (AMRAD) is a
nonprofit group of volunteers who have been working to find ways
to bring deaf data communicators into the new wave of technology,
and to interface microcomputers with communications devices for
the deaf.

In 1978, AMRAD established the fourth electronic message
system to be operational on the telephone lines in the United
States. It was the first bulletin board system to be also accessible over amateur radio through the use of five-bit Baudot-
coded signals. A similar bulletin board system, known as the
Virginia TTY, was set up separately to serve the deaf community
in the Washington, D.C., area. Later, a more sophisticated system
call HEX was brought on-line; it provided for ASCII-Baudot interchange and disk storage of messages which the smaller system
did not have. Hex is available to deaf callers using TTY standards at 301-593-7033.

AMRAD also has an active project underway to interface microcomputers acting as terminals with communications devices for the
deaf. The Apple II computer seems easy to interface, and several
demonstrations of this capability have been made. A simple interface device consisting of two ICs, some diodes, one transistor,
and a handful of resistors is connected to the Apple II game I/O
port.

The TRS-80 is more difficult to interconnect; $70 or more is
needed for parts alone to build a proper interface. Work has
also been done on PET/CBM, AIM 65, and other microcomputer systems.

Anyone interested in interfacing a microcomputer to communications systems for the deaf can contact AMRAD for more information at 1524 Springvale Avenue, McLean, Virginia 22101. Please remember that AMRAD is a volunteer, nonprofit organization. The organization has no products to sell and they can provide information only on an individual basis.

Novation has recently introduced a portable combination terminal/telephone aimed at the deaf market, called Infone.

Figure 10-1. Infone, a portable combination terminal/telephone designed for the deaf.

It has a store-and-forward message capability and is compatible with both ASCII and Baudot code. It also has the capability to "speak" in synthetic speech for blind users. Novation has designed Infone around a special "modem on a chip" which aids in keeping both size and cost down. The terminal can communicate through a direct connection to a standard modular telephone jack or via an optional acoustic modem.

The small desktop unit has a 2000-character memory expansible to 7000 for message storage, and 250-word vocabulary for synthesized speech. It uses a linear predictive coding chip from Texas Instruments.

Technology will continue to help deaf communicators in many ways in the coming years. It is already possible to put a microcomputer such as the TRS-80 Color Computer on-line as an ASCII terminal, with prepackaged hardware and software for around $500. As the value and popularity of data communications services grow, the price of mass-produced terminals will certainly drop even more. Deaf data communicators should be allowed to enjoy the services that come with microcomputer-based data communication systems, so they may interact with many new areas of society.

chapter eleven

Large Scale Communications Networks

This chapter will define and explain three different kinds of large scale communications networks. These networks have many similarities, in that they all consist of computers, transmission media, and private customers. Each kind of system emphasizes a different portion of the operation.

The three kinds of networks are information utilities, value-added carriers, and alternative telephone carriers. Information utilities place emphasis on their computing power and the size of their data base. Users call in over telephone systems and (as we shall see) value-added carriers, in order to use the computer. Information utilities include services such as the Source and CompuServe.

Value-added carriers often provide the links between the customers and many information utilities or computer utilities. They consist of local and network communications computers which move the users' data around efficiently and at high speed. The data from many customers can be packed into dedicated transmission systems at low cost. Additionally, the network computers detect and correct errors on the transmission link, and buffer and convert arriving data in various formats and speeds. The function of the network computers is invisible to the user. The emphasis is on carrying the data, not processing it.

Alternative telephone carriers provide competition for the large long distance telephone carriers which have had a near monopoly on telephone communications in the United States for many years. They use computers to route calls. A push-button telephone actually serves as a terminal device which tells the system computer who you are and where you want to talk. The emphasis is on carrying the communications again, but usually in terms of voice circuits.

Let us look at specific examples of each kind of system and see how they are related.

INFORMATION UTILITIES

Two major information utilities are available for the use of the general public in the United states. Many other systems are operational and highly successful in industry, education, and government, but the Source and CompuServe bring mainframe compu-

ting power to private users. Both systems have developed into
what might be considered electronic newspapers, but with different
formats.

The two systems have been competing in a very hectic horse-
race, and the public has been the winner. Each system brings new
features on-line almost daily, so it would be foolish to try to
list specifically their services. It is possible, however, to
generalize about the kinds of things you will find on both
systems, and the operating differences of each.

CompuServe and the Source both offer access to individuals
over standard local telephone lines. In most cases, a local call
is made to the regional terminal input point (TIP) of a value-
added carrier. The value-added carrier mixes the individual's
data in with that of possibly hundreds of other users and moves
it over high speed circuits to the large computer cluster of the
information utility.

The user may have two sign-on sequences: one for the value-
added carrier and one for the information utility itself. This
is a simple process involving the typing of a few characters and
letters. Calling an information utility is as easy as calling a
local ABBS in most metropolitan areas of the United States.
CompuServe provides its own direct lines to many major cities.
In smaller cities and rural areas, a long distance call may be
necessary to reach the nearest entry point. This factor should
always be considered when joining any information utility system,
because the coverage patterns are not identical and long distance
bills can add up quickly.

After sign-on, the user is greeted with announcements about
the system. These are very similar to headlines on the front page
of a newspaper. They may advertise new features, system news, or
important national news. The major operating difference between
Source and CompuServe becomes apparent after sign-on. CompuServe
is a menu-driven system; it uses the Teletex format. Users
select categories and subcategories of information from menus and
enter the number of the feature they would like to see. Compu-
Serve is simple for new users to operate because they are led
through a series of increasingly specific menus until they get
the desired information.

The Source will send a system prompt ( ) after the bulletins
and wait for the user to tell the system what to do. This system
is more flexible than a menu-driven format, and experienced users
can enter several stacked commands on one line; this brings quick
response. Menu-driven systems can exasperate experienced users
with their methodical presentation of each menu in its turn.

Both information utilities do a good job of presenting national news stories. Again, the more flexible entry format of
the Source allows experienced users to search for particular news
stories by key words, but the menu-driven format of CompuServe
allows easy browsing through lists of important stories which
might otherwise be missed.

Other features on the systems include business news, stock
reports, classified ads, seasonal specials, shopping (via the
catalogs of several different manufacturers), computer games, and
electronic mail. The electronic mail system of the Source is very
flexible in that it allows forwarding of mail, replying, and other
features. CompuServe's EMAIL is less flexible. Source mail will
accept an almost constant dump of characters from a prepared file.

EMAIL requires a terminal that transmits prestored messages in response to line-by-line prompts.

Both services provide the user with the ability to use the system as a more traditional time-shared computer. Various programming languages are available and large disk and RAM storage can be used at low daily rates. Programming aides and utilities, such as text editors, are available for persons using the higher order languages. Specific programs can be written on-line and saved, or any of the many programs in the system library can be selected and run. Use of the library programs and storage are extra cost options.

Each system is actually a cluster of computers. The Source operates on a group of Prime computers located in Maryland. The CompuServe service runs on a network of over twenty Digital Equipment Corporation mainframes in Ohio.

Most users will take advantage of the nonprime service hours of these systems. Nonprime service for CompuServe is 6:00 P.M. to 5:00 A.M. your local time and all day on Saturday, Sunday, and holidays. The Source has similar nonprime hours. Rates for nonprime time service run between five and seven dollars an hour. Prime time service (during the work day in your local area) can go higher than $20 an hour.

Terminal software for the most popular microcomputers is available from both the Source and CompuServe. CompuServe has cooperated closely with Radio Shack in integrating the Radio Shack Color Computer and other TRS-80 products into their system. The Videotex series of programs for the TRS-80 and Apple II microcomputers allows transmission of control codes and provides recognition of special cursor positioning and screen formatting commands. The program for the Color Computer allows transmission of messages prepared off-line.

The future of these information utility systems seems unlimited. They will continue to bring larger data bases and more unique features on-line. They have many options opening in the future for different ways of reaching their users. These options could include integration into cable television systems and possibly even direct satellite broadcast. Some microcomputer system users may seriously consider the balance between buying and maintaining a large microcomputer system and paying five to seven dollars per hour of evening use (plus optional services) for the almost unlimited computing power of a computer/information utility.

Before we leave these systems completely, there are two other systems you should know the names of, if only because they come up so often in reference. They are PLATO and the Arpanet.

PLATO is a time-shared system serving hundreds of colleges and universities throughout the country. Its main thrust is toward education and the use of computers in instruction. Hundreds of thousands of college students and faculty members have learned about some of the practical applications of data communications through PLATO. PLATO has served as a developmental base for many of the ideas we now incorporate in our data communication systems.

Similarly, the Arpanet developed data transmission techniques which are now the heart of modern data communication systems. "ARPA" is part of the acronym DARPA which stands for the Defense Advanced Research Projects Agency. DARPA is a small military agency which works at the leading edge of technology.

It saw the potential for data communications and established a developmental interactive computer network many years ago. The network is now administered by the Defense Communications Agency and is used by military agencies and contractors.

This network pioneered the packet switching technique which breaks strings of data into packets of information that are easily moved around in the transmission system. These packets can be routed in several different ways. Routing is done to insure the best utilization of all data trunks and to balance between them. When people write or talk about the Arpanet technology, they usually mean packet switching. Packet switching techniques are now being used by the next kind of communications network we will look at, the value-added carriers.

VALUE-ADDED CARRIERS

Let us begin with a quick primer on digital communications network switching techniques. You need to read through it if you are going to understand the packet switching techniques used by value-added carriers.

Picture a large data communications network as a telephone system. The major differences stem from the fact that data networks carry digital signals instead of analog voice messages. Each network has many subscribers linked together through a system of switching centers. In the telephone system, the switching centers switch calls based on the numbers dialed. The digital switches used in data networks may use different methods of switching data.

There are three kinds of digital switches: message switches, packet switches, and time-division circuit switches. Message switches came first and they are exemplified by the CBBS, ABBS, and Forum store-and-forward electronic message systems. A complete message comes in, is stored, then forwarded at the appropriate time to the appropriate recipient. The storage part of this process can take a long time and store-and-forward message switching can be a slow way to send a lot of messages. The next technology to be developed was packet switching. A "packet" of data is actually a string of characters. Packets can vary in size according to the design of the specific system. Some systems may use packets 2000 characters long. Two thousand characters may sound like a large message instead of a compact packet, but it is small compared to the huge streams of data transmitted by large computerized systems.

In packet switching, a block of data has addressing and possibly routing information added to it, so it can travel independently through an interconnected network of switches to its destination. Packets traveling independently through the system may arrive out of order at the destination, but they can be rearranged by the network's processors into the correct sequence. Some delays may take place while packets are being formed and addressed, and while they wait for each other to get through the system.

A third alternative in digital switching is called time-division circuit switching . These systems use very small blocks of data (even just one character) as their transmission element. They avoid adding addressing and routing information to this small data block by the use of signaling channels which are separate

from data channels. As the character or data block moves to a
switch, instructions go out on a separate line as to what to do
with it. The coded instructions are very simple and the data
channel is kept clear of all overhead. Time-division circuit
switching is a newer technique which has not been developed as
fully as packet switching.

Most of the value-added carriers today use some variation
of packet switching. Two packet-switched carriers are commonly
used to enter information utilities: TYMNET and GTE Telenet.
These carriers provide efficient transfer of data between large
computers, and between computers and customers' terminals. The
users make a local telephone call to enter the data network,
although large users will probably be connected to the network
through dedicated lines.

Each service has entry facilities in about 300 United States
cities. Service is concentrated in the urban areas of the east
and west coasts. Many rural areas may be without value-added
carrier services until satellite transmission facilities become
available. The services have extensions into Canada, Japan, and
Europe through international agreements.

The "value-added" service provided by value-added carriers
consists of two primary areas: detecting and correcting errors,
and matching different kinds of data communications formats together into a common network.

Error detection and correction removes and corrects "bad
bits" of data which were damaged or dropped during the transmission. The process relies heavily on statistical routines to
check literally millions of bits on a network every second.

The transparent interface feature of these networks allows
many different kinds of terminals using many different electrical
standards and coding schemes (there are probably over a dozen in
common use) to talk together without modification. The network's
translation features are invisible or transparent to the users.

The information utilities make use of TYMNET and Telenet to
carry the data between their mainframe computers and the individual users. Many casual communicators use these highly
sophisticated data transmission networks every time they dial an
information utility, yet they are not aware of the functions the
utility provides.

ALTERNATIVE TELEPHONE CARRIERS

Once there were only a couple of big telephone companies and a
smattering of small ones in the United States. They had the
country carved into different geographical areas and all services
they provided were billed according to tariffs set down by federal
and state regulatory agencies. Certain long-haul communications
carriers were chartered to interconnect the regional companies
into a national and worldwide telephone system. All these companies were regulated and well-protected. This monopoly was the
first and best (both in terms of quality and availability) telephone system in the world.

The monopolistic portion of the communications structure was
eventually challenged by companies who wanted to connect their own
equipment to telephone circuits. Private companies finally won
the right, through long and tough court fights, to compete in
various parts of the telephone market. Now, many types of FCC-

registered equipment are available which can be directly connected to the telephone lines--including modems.

Similarly, alternatives to the standard telephone carriers became available, but at first these services were only economical for large corporations who could benefit from saving a few cents on every call. This alternative form of telephone service became available to private individuals in many parts of the country in the early 1980s.

An alternative carrier network is really a system of voice circuits controlled by computer billing and switching systems. The voice circuits ride over microwave or satellite systems that may be owned by the alternative carrier or leased from yet another communications company. The circuits travel in large groups, perhaps with several conversations combined on each circuit through multiplexing techniques. These groups of circuits go from city to city. In each city, they connect to the existing local or metropolitan telephone system. This technique allows the alternative carriers to use high technology-low maintenance links between cities, while the local telephone companies provide the less glamorous, but very vital, local service to homes and businesses.

Users of alternative telephone services make calls in a two-step process. In the first step, they dial a local number to reach the alternative carrier's entry equipment. They then receive another, easily recognized, dial tone. In response to this signal, they enter a series of numbers using the push-button telephone dial. These numbers represent the customer account code. The area code and number of the party being called are also entered at this time. The alternative carrier system then routes the call over its own circuits to the city being called and re-dials the calls into the local telephone system. All this is done at a price that may be considerably less than normal long distance telephone service. Obviously, such a service would have great appeal to persons who want to dial into electronic message systems across the country.

There are two major alternative carriers offering service to private individuals. MCI Telecommunications and SP Communications offer two competing services. MCI uses the trademarked name Execunet, but they also refer to themselves as "The nation's long distance phone company." SP Communications calls their service Sprint.

Both services have similar (but not necessarily identical) billing schemes. Individual users pay a basic monthly service or subscription charge of around $10 to establish an account. They are then charged for each call according to the time of day, distance, and number of six-second time blocks used. Calls made during the daytime hours can cost as much as 30% less than those made on the more traditional carriers. The differences are less at the late night or weekend rates.

A prospective user of these alternative telephone systems have several factors to weigh. The primary factor is the geo-graphical area of coverage. Many cities and rural areas are not covered by this service. Remember, both the originating and terminating areas must be covered by the carrier for the call to go through. The monthly service fee must be considered as a part of each call made. During some times of the day and week-ends, the savings on a three-minute call across country may be as

little as a twenty-five cents. The savings may not offset the
service charge unless many calls are made. Additionally, the
standard telephone carriers may be able to provide Wide Area Telephone Service (WATS) rates if calls are often made to a specific
area. All of these factors must be considered but, generally, if
frequent calls are made on weekdays to metropolitan areas, these
alternative telephone services may save you a considerable amount
of money.

     One final note: the quality of the circuits provided by these
carriers may vary. They try to meet the highest standards of the
industry, but they lack the alternate routes and widespread maintenance base needed to allow constant line checking and maintenance.
Most data communicators have found the service perfectly adequate
for 300 baud service, but others have reported more frequent
errors when using these services for data communications. Most
problems can be worked out with the carrier.

THE NATIONAL NETWORKS

     All these network systems represent a tremendous potential
for the transfer of information and the interchange of ideas.
Their growth will continue to have great influence on the way we
learn, play, work, and shop. The future of the industrialized
countries of the world will be greatly influenced by communications networks. In the next chapter, we will look at the
future of data communications systems and networks.

chapter twelve

The Future

Predicting the future accurately can be a very difficult task. In the early 1950s predictions were made that personal helicopters were right around the corner and that commuters in the 1970s and 1980s would take off from their backyards and land on their office roofs. Scientists in the 1960s predicted colonies would be in space by the 1980s. Unfortunately, perhaps, these things have not happened. But the history of technological forecasting has many more examples of unforeseen developments than of wrong guesses. The things we can see usually happen in one form or another, and they happen faster than we believed possible. The things we cannot see far outnumber those we can. In this chapter, we will outline some developments that are reasonably easy to predict-- which probably means they are right around the corner.

TERMINALS

What developments will we see in the terminals over the next few years? The first development (demonstrated in the late 1970s) will be voice recognition and voice synthesis. Terminals will be able to recognize and act on voice commands--much as the special function keys today perform extended functions from the pressure on one key. More complex terminals, able to take dictation and provide highly reliable translation from spoken to written form, will be available by the end of the decade. Terminals and peripheral devices will also "talk" to their users. Perhaps they will only say a few standard words at first (perhaps "READY" will be the most common word a terminal speaks), but soon terminals will be able to speak every word as it appears on the screen. But even spoken interfacing has its limitations. The human/ machine barrier will eventually become totally transparent to the user. It is certain that an effective physiological or "bio-cybernetic" link between people and terminals will be developed. This link may not be as sophisticated as a mind implant--a favorite topic of science fiction writers--but it may be just as effective. Various kinds of sensors attached to the body can exchange stimulus messages with a computer. This stimulus can be translated by the operating system of the mind into meaningful information or physical shapes. Two variations of this process have already been successfully demonstrated.

Pilots of high performance fighter aircraft may have their vision blurred during high speed maneuvers, yet they still need to receive vital information. Warning horns and recorded women's voices have been used, but these sounds interfere with important radio messages. One system allows computers in the aircraft to communicate with the pilot through the use of a pulsed pressure cuff--similar to a blood pressure cuff--on the pilot's thigh. When the aircraft is near the edge of its performance envelope, the cuff begins to pulse with compressed air that is controlled by the aircraft's computerized flight system. The worse the condition of flight, the faster the rate of pulsation. Pilots quickly learn (are reprogrammed) to judge aircraft performance by the pressure on their leg. This is an easy and sure physiological communications link between a human pilot and a computer.

Another more complex example involves television images which are "seen" by blind people through pressure on their backs. The images from a television camera are changed to digital pulses; the pulses are fed through a computer which activates a device containing hundreds of tiny pins set in a rectangular pattern. This pin system can reproduce the television image by placing pressure on the pins to form an outline of the image. Blind persons can be trained to "see" the outline when the pin device is placed on open stretch of skin like the back. Continued training can lead to very accurate perception of objects in a kind of reprogrammed vision. This is another stimulating example of the kind of biocybernetic interface that can be developed with a little imagination. Other, more capable, links will certainly follow. The flexing of fingers during the operation of a keyboard is a learned physiological act, but there may be more effective physiological ways of receiving and putting information into a computer.

The real advantage of bioelectronic or physiological inter-faces is size. There are two major limitations on the size of a portable terminal: the power supply (batteries) and the I/O system (usually liquid crystal displays and push buttons). If the I/O system can be made invisible, great progress toward tiny portable terminals will be possible.

Certainly, the wrist terminal cannot be far away. There are already portable terminals under development which can interface with local radio systems for hospital and industrial work. The portable wrist-sized interactive terminal can become a reality in industry and medicine quickly.

Another major feature of desk-sized terminals will be exten-sive color graphics capabilities. Graphics systems will use digitized pictures of very high quality for a variety of purposes.

MESSAGE SYSTEMS

The trend in message systems will be for more features and inter-connection. Practical programs are under development which will allow one system to automatically dial another and transfer messages addressed to users of the called system. This would be the beginning of a true store-and-forward message service which could better the postal service for speed and cost (at low volume).

Higher speed transmission (1200 baud) using the Bell 212 modem standard will become common. The large memory storage capabilities of hard disks, and possibly even video disks, will

allow the use of programming languages and data storage rivaling
the present information utilities. Practical multiuser access
will also become common in systems serving large user populations.

INFORMATION UTILITIES AND NETWORKS

    Information utilities and value-added carriers will begin
to look even more alike as they take on each other's roles. Value-
added carriers are already offering such features as electronic mail service to their customers. Information utilities
will take advantage of satellite transmission capablities to
extend their services throughout the country and, therefore,
become their own carriers.
    Information utilities of all types will continue to prolif-
erate. Corporations will begin to offer access to information
utilities to all executives--not just to receive information, but
also to conduct business.
    Information utilities will continue to expand their on-line
data bases. The available data bases will rival community
libraries in research material and excel any other source of
current information. They will offer such services as digitized
voice and video. Voice synthesis terminals will tie to information utilities to read aloud the data presented on the screen.

A BEGINNING

   These predictions, like this book, are meant to stimulate you
to explore the world of data communications. Data communications
systems can allow your mind to travel out in the world and explore
new areas of knowledge and current events in a unique and interactive fashion. Your microcomputer can provide the key to the
door of knowledge and adventure. Come join us out on the data
network.

Appendix

ADDRESSES OF
MANUFACTURERS AND DISTRIBUTORS
OF DATA COMMUNICATIONS PRODUCTS

Anderson Jacobson   (Terminals, printers, and modems)
521 Charcot Avenue
San Jose, Calif. 95131

Apple Computer   (Computers)
10260 Bandley Drive
Cupertino, Calif. 95014
(408) 996-1010

ATARI   (Microcomputer systems, modems, software)
1265 Borregas Avenue
Dept. C
Sunnvale, Calif. 94086
(800) 538-8547

Bill Blue   (Message system software)
P.O. Box 1318
Lakeside, Calif. 92040
(714) 449-4222

CompuServe   (Information utility)
Personal Computing Division
500 Arlington Centre Boulevard
Columbus, Ohio 43220
(614) 457-8600

CP/M Users Group   (CP/M software)
1651 Third Avenue
New York, N.Y. 10028

Emtrol Systems   (Modems)
123 Locust Street
Lancaster, Pa. 17602
(717) 291-1116

GTE Telenet   (Value-added carrier)
8330 Old Courthouse Road
Vienna, Va.   22180
(703) 827-9200

Hazeltine Corp.   (Terminals)
10 East 53rd Street
New York, N.Y.   10022

Hayes Microcomputer Products   (Modems)
5835 Peachtree Corners East
Norcross, Ga.   30092

Heath Co.   (Computers)
Benton Harbor, Michigan   49022

Lear Siegler   (Terminals)
714 North Brookhurst Street
Anaheim, Calif.   92803

Lifeboat Associates   (CP/M operating system and programs)
1651 Third Avenue
New York, N.Y.   10028

Lindbergh Systems   (Software)
49 Beechmont Street
Worcester, Mass.   01609
(617) 799-2217

MCI Communications Corp.   (Alternative telephone service)
1150 17th Street, NW
Washington, D.C. 20036
(202) 872-1600

Microperipheral Corp.   (Modems and software)
P.O. Box 529
Mercer Island, Wash.   98040
(206) 454-3303

Microstuf Company   (Software for North Star and CP/M systems)
P.O. Box 33337
Decatur, Ga.   30033

MSI Date Corp.   (Portable terminals)
340 Fischer Avenue
Costa Mesa, Calif.   92626
(714) 549-6000

Nixdorf Computer   (Portable terminals)
168 Middlesex Turnpike
Burlington, Mass.   01803
(800) 225-1992

North Star Computers   (Microcomputers)
1440 Fourth Street
Berkeley, Calif.   94710

Novation   (Modems)
18664 Oxnard Street
Tarzana, Calif. 91356

Perkin-Elmer   (Terminals)
360 Route 206 South
Flanders, N.J. 07836

Potomac Micro-Magic   (Integrated S-100 modems)
P.O. Box 11149
Alexandria, Va. 22312
(703) 750-3727 (voice);
(703) 750-0930 (modem)

Small Business Systems Group   (ST80-communications software)
6 Carlisle Rd.
Westford, Mass. 01886
(617) 692-3800

Software Toolworks   (REACH software for H-89)
14478 Glorietta Drive
Sherman Oaks, Calif. 91423
(213) 986-4885

Software Sorcery   (ABBS software)
7927 Jones Branch Drive, Suite 400
McLean, Va. 22102
(703) 385-2944

Southwestern Data Systems   (Communications software)
10159-G Mission Gorge Road
Santee, Calif. 92071
(714) 562-3670

SP Communications   (Alternative telephone service)
P.O. Box 974
Burlingame, Calif. 94010
(415) 692-5600

TNW Corporation   (Hardware and software for Commodore/CBM)
3351 Hancock Street
San Diego, Calif. 92110

Tymnet   (Value-added carrier)
20665 Valley Green Drive
Cupertino, Calif. 95014
(408) 446-7000

Glossary

<u>ABBS</u>. Apple Bulletin Board System. An electronic message system based on the Apple II computer. Software written by Bill Blue and Craig Vaughan.

<u>ACK</u>. A positive acknowledgement control character.

<u>Acoustic coupler</u>. The portion of a modem which physically holds a telephone handset in two rubber cups.

<u>ANSI</u>. American National Standards Institute. Accepts standards for codes, alphabets, and signaling schemes.

<u>ASCII</u>. American Standard Code for Information Interchange. More correctly known as USASCII because of some changes in recent versions. A method of coding digital signals. The ASCII character contains seven bits; an eighth parity bit is often needed.

<u>Asynchronous</u>. A method of transmission in which the characters are not required to be in perfect timing. Start and stop bits are added to coordinate the transfer of characters.

<u>Baud</u>. A measure of transmission speed. The reciprocal of the time duration of the shortest signal element in a transmission. In RS-232-C ASCII transmission the signal element is one bit.

<u>Baudot code</u>. A coding scheme for data transmission using a five-bit (five-level) code. Still used in communications systems for the deaf. The code now known as "Baudot" was really written by Donald Murray and replaced the older Baudot scheme. It is now sometimes known as the Murray code. CCITT alphabet Number 2.

<u>BCD</u>. A coding scheme using a six-bit (six-level code).

<u>Bell 103</u>. Modem protocol using four tones for full-duplex operation on a single channel. Usually limited to 300 baud.

Bell 113. Modem portocol identical to Bell 103 above.

Bell 202. Modem protocol using two tones for half-duplex transmission. Maximum speed on dialed circuits is 1200 baud. The mark tone equals 1200 Hz, and the space tone equals 2200 Hz.

Bell 212. A dual mode modem protocol featuring full-duplex transmission of speeds up to 300 baud using the 103 protocol or up to 1200 baud using a phase shifted carrier. Not compatible with 202 type devices.

Bit. Smallest unit of information. In digital signaling, commonly refers to a change in state between 0 and 1.

Block. A number of characters transmitted as a group.

BPS. Bits per second.

Buffer. A temporary storage space, usually in RAM.

Byte. A group of eight bits.

CBBS. Computer Bulletin Board System. An electronic message system based on S-100 bus hardware and the CP/M operating system. Developed by Ward Christensen and Randy Suess.

CCITT. Consultive Committee International Telegraph and Telephone. A committee of the United Nations which accepts international standards.

Character. One letter, number, or special code.

Common carrier. Transmission companies (telephone, and so on) that serve the general public.

Control character. A character used for special signaling. Often not printed or displayed, but causing special functions such as screen clear, printer tab, and so on.

CPU. Central Processing Unit.

CPS. Characters Per Second.

Current loop. An electrical interface that is sensitive to current changes as opposed to voltage swings. Often used with older teleprinter equipment.

Cursor. The point of light indicating the place on a video screen where the the next character will appear.

DB-25. The designation of the standard plug and jack set used in RS-232-C wiring. Twenty-five pin connectors with thirteen pins on the top and twelve pins on the bottom row.

DCE. Data Communications Equipment. A common designation for communications equipment such as computers and modems. Uses a female DB-25 chassis jack.

DTE. Data Terminal Equipment. A common designation for communications equipment such as printers and terminals. Uses a male DB-25 chassis plug.

EBCDIC. Extended Binary Coded Decimal Interchange Code. An eight-bit code used primarily on IBM business systems.

Echo-plex. A method of transmission in which characters are echoed from the distant end and the echoes are presented on the terminal.

Echo suppressor. A device used to eliminate the echo effect of long distance voice transmission circuits. These suppressors must be disabled for full-duplex data transmission. The modem answer tones turn the suppressors off automatically.

EIA. Electronic Industries Association.

FCC. Federal Communications Commission.

Forum 80. An electronic message system based on the TRS-80 hardware. Software written by Bill Abney.

FSK. Frequency Shift Keying. A transmission method using two different frequencies--like a modem.

Full-duplex. The ability to talk both ways at the same time.

Half-duplex. Alternating transmissions--like CB ("over").

Handshaking. Exchange of control codes or specific characters to control the data flow.

Interface. The interconnection point--usually between equipment.

I/O. Input/Output.

K. Abbreviation for Kilo, meaning 1000; for example, an 8K memory has 8000 bytes of storage.

KSR. Keyboard Send and Receive, or a terminal with a keyboard.

Mark. A signaling condition equal to a binary 1.

Message switching. A switching technique using a message store-and-forward system.

Modem. Modulator and Demodulator. A device which translates between electrical signals and audio tones. The audio tones may be used over telephone or radio circuits.

NAK. A control code indicating that a character or block of data was not received.

Network. A communications system made up of various stations.
The phrase network assumes interaction between the stations.

On-line. Connected to a network or host computer system.

Parallel transmission. Simultaneous transmission of all the bits
in a byte down eight parallel wires.

Parity. A check of the total number of one-bits in a character.
In ASCII, a final eight bit is set so the count, when transmitted,
is either always even or always odd. This even or odd state can
easily be checked at the receiving end.

PMS. People's Message System. An electronic message system based
on Apple II hardware. Software written by Bill Blue.

Protocol. A set of rules governing the transmission of information over a data channel.

Reverse Channel. An "answer back" channel provided during half-
duplex operation. Allows the receiving modem to send low speed
acknowledgements to the transmitting modem without breaking the
half-duplex mode.

RAM. Random Access Memory.

ROM. Read Only Memory.

RS-232-C. An electrical standard for the interconnection of
equipment established by the Electronic Industries Association.
Practically identical to CCITT recommendation V. 24.

SNA. Systems Network Architecture. A local networking scheme
developed by IBM.

Space. The signal condition that equals a binary zero.

Start bit. A data bit used in asynchronous transmission to signal
the beginning of a character.

Stop bit. A data bit used in asynchronous transmission to signal
the end of a character and an idle channel. A mark condition
lasting longer than the normal data bit.

Store-and-forward. A system, usually used in message switching,
where messages are held until the appropriate receiving party is
available.

Synchronous. A transmission system in which characters are
synchronized by the transmission of initial synch characters.
No stop or start bits are used.

WPM. Words Per Minute.

Index

Now...Announcing These Other Fine Books From Spectrum!

THE ESSENTIAL COMPUTER DICTIONARY AND SPELLER, By Charles Sippl.
A handy reference that is invaluable for anyone who is involved
with computers. Sippl provides a reliable source of both
spellings and meanings of more than 10,000 words. This is a
reference that you'll turn to time and time again.
  ☐$6.95 paperback (284356)   ☐$14.95 hardback (284364)

TRS-80 DATA COMMUNICATIONS SYSTEMS, By Frank J. Derfler, Jr.
For TRS-80 users, here is Derfler's latest book. The guide
explains communications with the TRS-80 as the primary microcomputer.
  ☐$12.95 paperback (931220)   ☐$22.95 hardback (931228)

COMPUTER PROGRAMS IN BASIC, By Paul Friedman. A fully indexed
guide to over 1,600 BASIC computer programs covering six major
discipline fields of Business/Finance, Games, Math, Science/
Education, Personal Interest, and Utility. This directory
provides program reviews in over 173 categories and describes
what the program does, where it can be found, and lists the
equipment needed to make the program run. An excellent reference!
  ☐$10.95 paperback (165217)   ☐$19.95 hardback (165255)

     You can obtain these and other Spectrum Books at your local
     bookstore or you can use the order form below.

     Please send me the books I've checked above.
     Enclosed is my check or money order for   _____

         Yes, please send me the Spectrum Catalog of all
     your fine books   ____.50
     Please add 50¢ per book for postage and handling.   _____

     TOTAL   _____

     Name...
     Address..
     City.........................State............Zip.........

     Cut out and mail this form to: Prentice-Hall, Inc.
                                     Spectrum Books
                                     ATT D. K. Michaels
                                     Englewood Cliffs, N.J. 07632

     Prices subject to change without notice. Please allow 4
     weeks for delivery.

                    Spectrum  Books